Crystal Play

Crystal Play

Fun & Fabulous Designs for Stitched Jewelry

Anna Elizabeth Draeger

KALMBACH BOOKS

Kalmbach Books
21027 Crossroads Circle
Waukesha, Wisconsin 53186
www.Kalmbach.com/Books

Published in 2013

17 16 15 14 13   1 2 3 4 5

Manufactured in the United States of America

ISBN: 978-0-87116-476-6
EISBN: 978-0-87116-781-1

Editor: Mary Wohlgemuth
Art director: Lisa Bergman
Technical editor: Jane Danley Cruz
Layout designer: Lisa Schroeder
Photographer: James Forbes
Illustrator: Kellie Jaeger

Library of Congress Cataloging in Publication Data
Draeger, Anna Elizabeth.
   Crystal play : fun & fabulous designs for stitched jewelry / Anna Elizabeth Draeger.

      p. : col. ill. ; cm.

   Issued also as an ebook.
   ISBN: 978-0-87116-476-6

   1. Beadwork–Handbooks, manuals, etc. 2. Beadwork–Patterns. 3. Jewelry making. I. Title.

TT860 .D732 2013
745.594/2

Contents

Come play in my world

The ever-changing world of crystal beads is my constant inspiration, and this collection of jewelry designs is the result of playing with some of the latest products available from *Swarovski Elements*. The company releases new colors, shapes, and finishes twice a year, and as one of Swarovski's *Create Your Style* Ambassadors, I'm fortunate to get product samples as soon as they're available so I can design with them as inspiration strikes me.

I wear my jewelry all the time because—when you think about it—every day is special.

Right after I finished my first book, *Crystal Brilliance*, I knew that I'd want to write another book that showcases crystal jewelry. My first book features 26 jewelry designs in four design categories: Classic, Romantic, Geometric, and Organic. For this book, I decided to shake things up and have a little more fun.

This book has four project chapters: Beaded Beads, Component Craze, Playful Favorites, and Another Dimension. Each has unexpected twists that give them a fun or even funky spin. Many of the designs in this book can be used as accessories for special occasions, but I wear my jewelry all the time because—when you think about it—every day is special.

NEW DIRECTIONS

Have you ever discovered a new, extraordinary crystal component and had no clue how to incorporate it into your beadwork? (I have too, every so often.) That's where the designs in this book will be helpful: They'll clue you in to my

design process, and you can stitch up the project as I did or let it spark new ideas of your own. I incorporate some new components that you didn't see in my first book, such as the pendant shape in the Woven Crystal Clusters Bracelet.

You'll notice a few other materials that are unusual and exciting when paired with crystals: Czech-made Picasso-finish beads, for example. I used them to line the Snake-Belly Bangle with a cool interior that lives up to its name. Playing with inspiring materials always helps me create a fabulous finished product.

MY DESIGN PROCESS AND FAVORITE STITCHES

My favorite beaded designs are usually a result of taking the time to spread out materials and try different combinations—basically, make a mess of my work area, just like I did as a kid in my backyard. Little details always caught my attention. It's no wonder I was drawn to beadwork.

I enjoy mixing different stitches in my designs. You'll find all my favorites used here: herringbone, St. Petersburg chain, right-angle weave, and peyote stitch, to name a few. Most of these stitches are explained within the project directions. If you are unfamiliar with a stitch or need a quick lesson on things like adding a stop bead or zipping up peyote ends, check out the Basics Review at the end of the book.

"PLAYTIME" OPTIONS

Readers loved the bonus of getting an alternate design idea in my first crystal book, so you'll see that feature again in this book. This time it's called "Playtime" in the hopes that you'll stretch your creative thinking along with me and look at the main project in a different way.

I created these variations by allowing myself the freedom to play around with the design of the main project without worrying too much about the end result (at least at first). I switched out beads or used an element of the design as a component or in another way (such as in a pair of earrings or creating a necklace from a bracelet design). The look can change drastically without changing much in the way of materials or technique. Maybe you'll come up with playful options of your own.

COLOR CHOICES

I love colors that are soothing, one flowing right into the next. I often work in greens, blues, and purples—cool colors—and my colors tend to be analogous (they sit next to each other on the color wheel). I like a monochromatic color scheme as well, which features different values, or intensities, of the same hue. In this book, I challenged myself to include some new finishes and more-neutral color schemes as in the Beehive Bangle and Snake-Belly Bangle.

You will find Swarovski's color names for the crystal components I use in the materials lists. Often I hear fans of my work say they want to make a project using the exact colors I did, down to the last seed bead, and then they drive themselves crazy hunting down colors that may be hard to find or even discontinued. My suggestion? Let go of the idea of having to make an exact replica. Bead colors get discontinued all the time and new colors are added.

Readers **loved** the bonus of getting an **alternate design idea** in my first crystal book, so you'll see that feature again in this book.

You'll find all **my favorite stitches** used here: crossweave, St. Petersburg chain, right-angle weave, and peyote stitch, to name a few.

Of all the crystal shapes available, the **bicone** is definitely my **number-one** choice.

I also love to work with *Swarovski Elements* crystal pearls, which are beautifully perfect imitations of natural pearls. A spherical crystal core gives crystal pearls the weight of real pearls, and they are available in many gorgeous colors. The holes are consistent and larger than those in natural pearls, so they are easy to incorporate into stitching projects. Each pearl in the strand is perfectly consistent with the next.

To help avoid frustration and encourage you to explore what you think looks best (or use what you have on hand), I use generic terms like "dark green" or "metallic blue."

CRYSTAL SHAPES AND SIZES

Of all the crystal shapes available, the bicone is definitely my number-one choice. As in my first book, most of the designs in this book feature bicone crystals. Bicones are versatile, economical, and quintessential crystal beads. The Xilion, the patented bicone crystal shape from the *Swarovski Elements* line, is even more sparkly than the traditional bicone crystal, and can be used whenever bicones are called for.

SEED BEADS, BUGLES, AND CYLINDERS

To supplement the sparkling crystals and the occasional pearl, I usually choose seed beads, bugles, and cylinder beads. Occasionally I use unusual bead shapes, such as the new SuperDuos (twin beads). I prefer the consistency of Japanese-made beads, and that's what I used in the projects. I like precise, smooth stitches in my jewelry, and using consistent beads helps create an even look. Czech beads, which usually are sold on hanks, give a more uneven texture to beadwork (which sometimes is desirable).

Choose your beads carefully, discarding any misshapen beads or crystals with rough edges. This is called culling. If a seed bead is lopsided, discard it. If a bugle bead has a broken edge or is shorter than the others, discard it. Always use the best quality to create the finest jewelry.

FINDINGS

My first choice is to use sterling silver or gold-filled findings. Many quality findings made of base (nonprecious) metals are available, and I sometimes use these in my work. Base metals cause skin reactions for some people; consider this if you give your jewelry as gifts.

To attach clasps to the ends of beading wire, I prefer crimp tubes to crimp beads for a professional look. Again, I use precious metal crimps—sterling silver and gold-filled—which are easier to crimp and hold up better than base metal crimps. I also like to use 3mm crimp covers for a finishing touch in my jewelry.

NEEDLES

Long beading needles are my favorite; I suggest you keep numbers 10, 12, and 13 in your stash. Of these, #10s are the biggest, and they are the easiest to thread. If you find they are too big to fit through certain beads, you can always switch to a thinner needle.

BEADING THREAD

Fireline is my favorite thread. This super-strong polyethylene fiber stands up very well to the sharp edges of crystals and bugles. It has no stretch, so your beadwork will not loosen with wear. Most often I use 6 lb. test; a common range for beading is 4–8 lb. test. I usually use the color called Smoke because it works well with most medium- to dark-colored beads. Another color option in Fireline is Crystal; it works well with light-colored crystals and beads. Some suppliers offer Fireline in a variety of dyed colors so you can match your bead color. All the projects in the book call for Fireline, but you may substitute your favorite beading thread.

to lose beads or watch as all of your hard work comes undone. When you're down to about 6–8 in. (15–20cm) of thread, weave back through the beadwork just finished, crossing the thread over itself if possible, following the same thread path and tying a few half-hitch knots as you go. The weaving is more important than the knots; it locks the thread in place and secures the end.

Take time to end your project properly, because rushing this step will waste all the time you spend creating if your work ends up falling apart. My favorite solution is to incorporate a beaded clasp as a finishing touch. If I use a purchased clasp, I don't sew it directly to the project; instead, I make a loop of seed beads and use jump rings to connect the two.

THREAD TENSION

Try to maintain even, moderately tight tension as you work. The way you hold your work will affect your tension. After you pull a stitch through, hold the thread with your thumb and index finger where the thread exits the last bead. Keep holding until you work the next stitch and pull a new thread through. That way, the previous stitch can't loosen before the next is completed. You can always go back and retrace a thread path if you can't seem to get the right tension the first time around. It's much easier to pull everything tight when the beads are

Keep your working length of thread manageable—I suggest no more than an arm's length or two. I usually work with a single thread. Keep the needle near the end of your working thread. The point where the eye of the needle sits will be a weak spot in the thread and can compromise your beadwork. Also, the more thread you pull through the needle, the more likely it is to tangle and knot.

BEGINNING AND ENDING THREAD

You may need to start a new thread before you complete a bracelet project, and most certainly as you're stitching a necklace. You don't want already in place. Using the right tension will minimize the amount of thread showing. Some stitches (herringbone in particular) are more prone to exposed thread—it's just the nature of the stitch. With stitches like that, be extra-careful to match thread color to the bead color.

STRETCHING AND STRENGTHENING

I live with painful tendinitis, and I want to stress how important it is to take care of your hands. Stretch your fingers every so often as you bead. Take frequent breaks and use ergonomic tools. Stand up, walk around, and stretch at intervals.

Try to maintain good posture while you work as well. Strengthening your core muscles will help you sit up straight as you work. As long as you haven't yet developed any problems, you can practice preventative stretching (check with your doctor first if you have questions).

Take frequent breaks and use ergonomic tools. Stand up, walk around, and stretch at intervals.

WORK AREA

A soft work surface will help you have pleasant and productive beading sessions. You want a surface large enough to spread out all your beads and beadwork. I use a large piece of Vellux on my beading table or a portable lap desk. Keep the area around you clear of anything that can snag your working thread.

Make sure you have proper lighting. It will help you work for longer stretches, save eyestrain, and help you catch errors early. I use a floor lamp with a full-spectrum bulb positioned directly over my work tray, and I flood the room with as much light as possible. Natural light is always my first choice.

MY WISH FOR READERS

As you use this book, I hope you are inspired to try new ideas, change my patterns to suit your tastes, and use your favorite materials and colors. It is one of my greatest joys to share designs that keep people creating art with their hands.

Beaded Beads

Perfect Beaded Beads

Cubic right-angle weave is the template for these classically styled, fun-to-make beaded beads. Choose whether to showcase pearls or crystals in a bold beaded pendant or a pretty set of beads for a necklace.

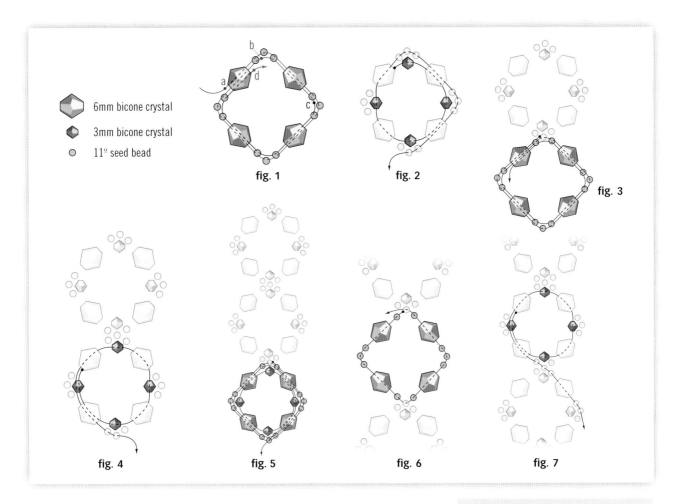

fig. 1

fig. 2

fig. 3

fig. 4

fig. 5

fig. 6

fig. 7

◇ 6mm bicone crystal

◆ 3mm bicone crystal

○ 11º seed bead

1 On 2 yd. (1.8m) of Fireline, pick up a pattern of a 6mm bicone crystal and three 11º seed beads four times. Sew back through the first 6mm and the first 11º picked up, leaving a 6-in. (15cm) tail **[fig. 1, a–b]**.

2 Skip the center 11º and sew through the next 11º, 6mm, and 11º **[b–c]**. Repeat two times, skip the next 11º, and then sew through the beadwork to exit a 6mm **[c–d]**.

3 Pick up a 3mm bicone crystal, and sew through the next 6mm. Repeat three times, and then sew through the beadwork to exit a center 11º. This completes one side of the cube **[fig. 2]**.

(The 3mms can be tucked under the seed beads or can sit on top. If you want them on top, position them as you work, or pick up five 11ºs between the 6mms on the sides instead of three.)

4 To begin the second side, pick up an 11º and a pattern of a 6mm and three 11ºs three times, and then pick up a 6mm and an 11º. Sew back through the center 11º in the previous side, and sew through the ring of beads again, skipping the center 11ºs of the new side. Exit a 6mm **[fig. 3]**.

5 Repeat step 3, adding 3mms between the 6mms. Exit a center 11º opposite the 11º connecting the first two sides **[fig. 4]**.

6 Repeat steps 4 and 5 to make a third side **[fig. 5]**.

7 To make the fourth side, connect the first and third sides. Pick up an 11º, a 6mm, three 11ºs, a 6mm, and an 11º. Sew through the center 11º from the first side. Repeat the sequence and sew through the center 11º from the third side **[fig. 6]**.

8 Reinforce and add 3mms to the fourth side as you did for the other three sides. Exit a center 11º along the edge of one of the sides **[fig. 7]**.

MATERIALS
Amethyst crystal bead 26mm
- **24** 6mm bicone crystals (Swarovski, amethyst)
- **36** 3mm bicone crystals (Swarovski, indicolite AB 2X)
- 3 grams 11º seed beads (teal)
- Fireline 6 lb. test
- Beading needles, #12 or #13

Green pearl bead
- 6mm pearls (Swarovski, green)
- 3mm bicone crystals (Swarovski, chrysolite)
- 11º cylinders (metallic green)

Blue bead
- 6mm helix crystals (aquamarine)
- 3mm bicone crystals (tanzanite)
- 11º seed beads (silver-lined light blue)

Pink pearl bead
- 5mm pearls (Swarovski, antique pink)
- 3mm bicone crystals (Swarovski, light rose satin)
- 11º cylinders (pink)

9 The top of the bead will have four open center 11ºs. These are the points where the top will be added. Pick up an 11º, a 6mm, and an 11º. Sew through the center 11º of the next side. Repeat three times [**fig. 8**]. Sew through the next 11º and 6mm.

10 Add 3mms to the top as you did for the sides [**fig. 9**], and reinforce. Sew through the beadwork to exit a bottom center 11º, and add the bottom of the bead as you did the top.

11 Add three 3mms at each corner of the beaded bead, where the sides meet [**fig. 10**]. End the threads.

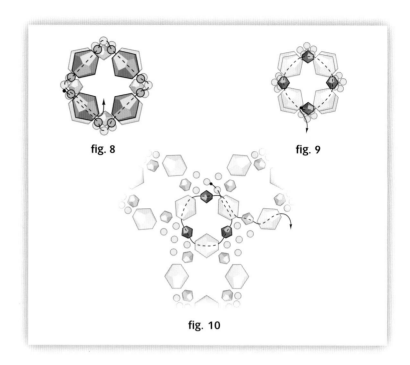

fig. 8

fig. 9

fig. 10

Playtime

Make small beaded beads that could easily be used as bracelet or earring components: Use 3mm pearls in place of the 6mm bicone crystals, 2mm round crystals in place of the 3mm bicone crystals, and 15º seed beads in place of the 11ºs. For fun, I tried 8mm twisted pearls and loved the unusual look they created.

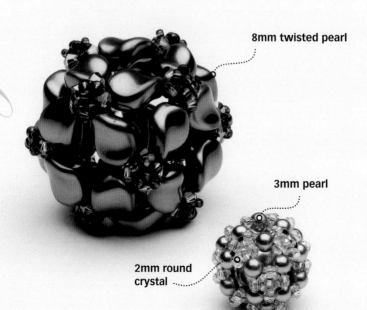

8mm twisted pearl

3mm pearl

2mm round crystal

COLORS
Black pearl bead
- 8mm twisted pearls (Swarovski, black)
- 3mm bicone crystals (Swarovski, crystal satin)
- 11º seed beads (silver-lined dark purple)

Green pearl bead
- 3mm pearls (Swarovski, green)
- 2mm round crystals (Swarovski, crystal moonlight)
- 15º seed beads (gilt-lined opal)

Bugle-Bead Bracelet

Using the same cubic right-angle weave technique as in the first project, substitute bugle beads for the sides and fill in the spaces with crystal crosses. The smaller the bugle beads, the smaller the overall bead, so you'll be able to stitch cute components for all types of jewelry. Use large bugle beads to showcase large crystals or patterned sides.

MATERIALS

For one bead 19mm
- **24** 6mm twisted bugle beads (silver-lined light green AB)
- **24** 4mm bicone crystals (Swarovski, jet AB 2X)
- **2 grams** 11º seed beads (teal)
- **2 grams** 15º seed beads (light green)
- Fireline 6 lb. test
- Beading needles, #13

Bracelet 8¼ in. (21cm)
- **9** beaded beads
- **10** 8mm bicone crystals (Swarovski, indicolite)
- Clasp
- **2** crimp beads
- **2** crimp covers
- Beading wire, .014
- Crimping pliers
- Wire cutters

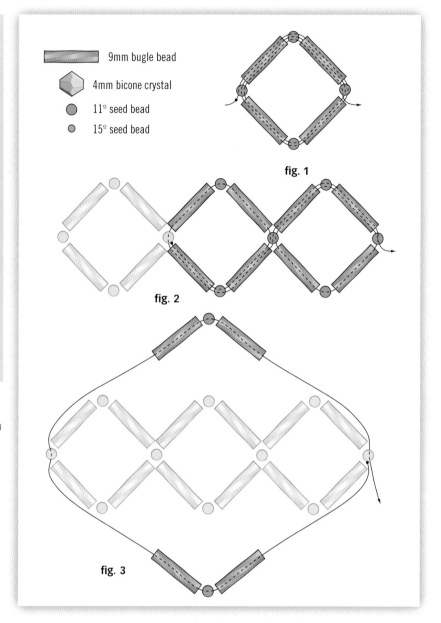

9mm bugle bead

4mm bicone crystal

11º seed bead

15º seed bead

fig. 1

fig. 2

fig. 3

1 On 1 yd. (.9m) of Fireline, pick up a pattern of an 11º seed bead and a 6mm bugle bead four times, leaving a 10-in. (25cm) tail. Sew through all the beads again to create a diamond shape, and exit an 11º opposite the tail **[fig. 1]**.

2 Pick up a pattern of a bugle bead and an 11º three times, and then pick up a bugle bead. Sew through the 11º your thread exited at the start of the step and sew through all the beads in the new diamond again. Exit the end 11º opposite the join. Repeat this step for a third diamond **[fig. 2]**.

3 Connect the first and third diamond to make a fourth diamond: Pick up a bugle bead, an 11º, and a bugle bead. Sew through the end 11º of the first diamond. Pick up a bugle bead, an 11º, and a bugle bead. Sew through the end 11º of the third diamond **[fig. 3]**. Retrace the thread path through all the beads in the fourth diamond.

4 There are four open 11ºs along one edge of the ring and four open 11ºs along the other edge. Sew through a bugle bead and an edge 11º on either side of the ring.

5 Pick up a bugle bead, and sew through the next open 11º along this edge of the ring. Repeat this stitch three more times to create a diamond shape along this edge **[fig. 4]**. Retrace the thread path through the new diamond shape, exit an 11º, and set the working thread aside.

6 Using the tail, sew through the beadwork to exit an open 11º along the other edge of the ring, and repeat step 5. End the tail.

7 Using the working thread, pick up a 15º seed bead, a 4mm bicone crystal, an 11º, a 4mm, and a 15º. Sew through the next 11º in the same diamond shape, back through all the beads just picked up, and back through the 11º your thread exited at the start of this step. Sew through the first 15º, 4mm, and 11º picked up in this step **[fig. 5]**.

8 Pick up a 4mm and a 15º. Sew through the opposite 11º in the diamond shape, back through the 15º and 4mm just picked up, and back through the center 11º **[fig. 6]**.

9 Pick up a 4mm and a 15º, and sew through the remaining 11º in this diamond shape. Sew back through the 15º and 4mm

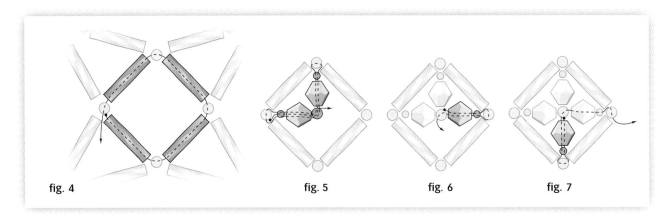

fig. 4　　**fig. 5**　　**fig. 6**　　**fig. 7**

just picked up, the center 11º, and the 4mm and 15º picked up in the previous step, and exit the 11º in the diamond shape **[fig. 7]**.

10 Repeat steps 7–9 to complete the crystal embellishment on the remaining diamond shapes. End the working thread.

11 Make a total of nine beaded beads.

12 On one end of 12 in. (30cm) of beading wire, string a crimp bead and half of a clasp. Go back through the crimp bead and crimp it.

13 String a pattern of an 8mm bicone crystal and a beaded bead until all the beaded beads are strung. Pick up an 8mm, a crimp bead, and the remaining half of the clasp. Go back through the crimp bead and crimp it.

14 Place a crimp cover over each crimp bead, and close.

Use different sizes of seed beads and crystals to make bigger or smaller beads. To make the crystal embellishments in the large bead, I picked up 12mm bugle beads in place of 6mm bugle beads. In step 7, pick up a 3mm, a 15º, a 3mm, a 15º, a 3mm, a 15º, and a 3mm, and sew through to exit the center 15º. In steps 8 and 9, pick up a 3mm, a 15º, and a 3mm.

COLORS
Large bead
- 12mm bugle beads (nickel)
- 3mm bicone crystals (Swarovski, garnet satin)
- 11º and 15º seed beads (nickel)

Small bead
- 6mm bugle beads (black)
- 4mm bicone crystals (Swarovski, fuchsia)
- 11º and 15º seed beads (black)

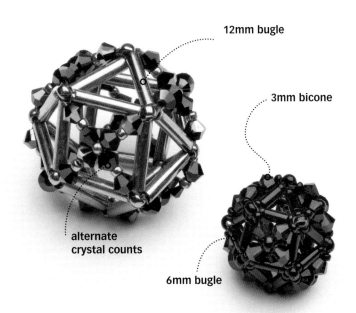

12mm bugle

3mm bicone

alternate crystal counts

6mm bugle

Wonky Beaded Beads

Rounded stitches of right-angle weave worked into a zigzag base roll up into a not-quite-round, charmingly wonky little bead. The pattern can also be worked as a long strip to create a bracelet.

MATERIALS
Bead #1 (pacific green) 18mm
- **20** 4mm round crystals (Swarovski, palace green opal)
- **6** 4mm rondelle crystals (Swarovski, pacific opal)
- 1–2 grams 11º seed beads (silver-lined light blue AB)
- Fireline 6 lb. test
- Beading needles, #12

COLORS
Bead #2 (light azore)
- 4mm bicone crystals (Swarovski, light azore)
- 4mm rondelle crystals (Swarovski, pacific opal)
- 15º seed beads (gunmetal)

Bead #3 (tanzanite)
- 4mm bicone crystals (Swarovski, tanzanite AB 2X)
- 11º seed beads (transparent teal)

Bead #4 (dark gray pearl)
- 3mm round pearls (Swarovski, dark gray)
- 4mm round crystals (Swarovski, Bermuda blue)
- 11º seed beads (metallic silver)

Bead #5 (pacific opal)
- 5mm bicone crystals (Swarovski, pacific opal)
- 4mm bicone crystals (Swarovski, light sapphire)
- 11º seed beads (transparent teal)

Bead #6 (purple pearl)
- 4mm round pearls and 3mm bicone crystals (Swarovski, purple and violet)
- 3mm bicone crystals (Swarovski, purple velvet)
- 11º seed beads (silver-lined violet)

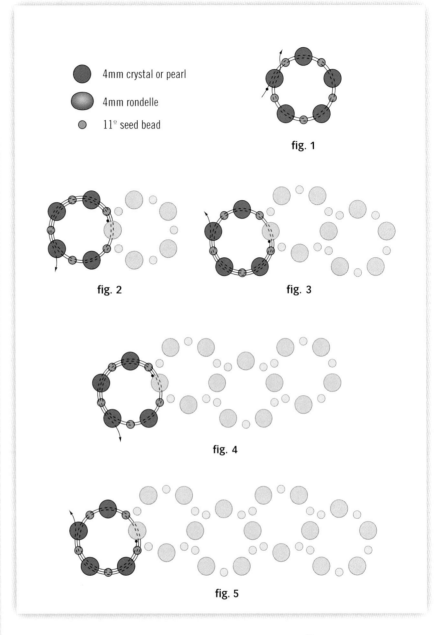

4mm crystal or pearl

4mm rondelle

11º seed bead

fig. 1

fig. 2

fig. 3

fig. 4

fig. 5

1 On 2 yd. (1.8m) of Fireline, pick up a pattern of a 4mm round crystal and an 11º seed bead five times, leaving a 12-in. (30cm) tail. Sew through all the beads again to form a ring, and exit the first 4mm picked up [**fig. 1**].

2 Pick up a pattern of an 11º and a 4mm four times, and then pick up an 11º. Sew through the 4mm your thread exited at the start of this step, and then retrace the thread path of the new ring. (If you don't do this, your bead will be floppy.) Sew through six beads past the 4mm that connects the two rings [**fig. 2**].

3 Repeat step 2 [**fig. 3**].

4 Repeat step 2, sewing through six beads past the connecting 4mm [**fig. 4**].

5 Repeat step 4 [**fig. 5**].

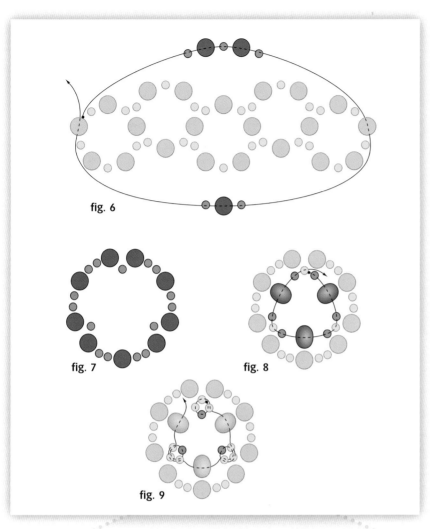

fig. 6

fig. 7

fig. 8

fig. 9

6 Connect the strip in a ring: Pick up a pattern of an 11º and a 4mm twice, then pick up an 11º. Skip an 11º, a 4mm, and an 11º on the opposite end ring, and sew through the next 4mm. Pick up an 11º, a 4mm, and an 11º, and sew through the 4mm your thread exited on the other end ring **[fig. 6]**. Retrace the thread path through the connecting ring, and sew through the next 11º, 4mm, and 11º of the connecting ring.

7 Along one edge, the beads will be in the pattern shown **[fig. 7]**. Pick up an 11º, a 4mm rondelle crystal, and an 11º. Skip seven beads along the edge, and sew through the following 11º between the two edge 4mms. Repeat twice **[fig. 8]**.

8 Exiting an 11º along the edge, sew through the next 11º, pick up an 11º, and sew through the nearest 11º to create a picot between two of the 4mm rondelles picked up in the previous step. Repeat twice **[fig. 9]**. Reinforce the new rondelle ring several times, and set the working thread aside.

9 Thread a needle on the tail and repeat steps 7 and 8 along the other edge of the bead. End the tail. If you are satisfied with the tension of the stitching, end the working thread; otherwise, use the remaining thread to reinforce the beadwork, and then end the working thread.

Playtime

Use top-drilled bicone crystals to make a spiky version. I used all 6mm top-drilled bicone crystals in place of the 4mm round crystals, and 8º seed beads in place of the 11º seed beads.

6mm
top-drilled
bicone

COLORS
• 6mm top-drilled bicone crystals (Swarovski, violet)
• 8º seed beads (metallic blue)

Sweet Beaded-Bead Bracelet

Tiny seed bead sides support the smallest crystals in these terrific little components, which I've strung together in a bracelet. Two make a cute pair of earrings; stitch up a few more for a lovely necklace.

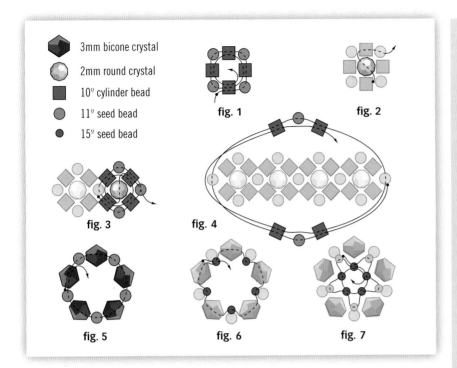

3mm bicone crystal
2mm round crystal
10º cylinder bead
11º seed bead
15º seed bead

fig. 1

fig. 2

fig. 3

fig. 4

fig. 5

fig. 6

fig. 7

MATERIALS
For one bead 11mm
- **10** 3mm bicone crystals (Swarovski, olivine)
- **5** 2mm round crystals (Swarovski, garnet)
- **20** 10º cylinder beads (olive-lined AB)
- **15** 11º seed beads (olive-lined AB)
- **20** 15º seed beads (gold-lined AB)
- Fireline 6 lb. test
- Beading needles, #12

Bracelet 8¼ in. (21cm)
- **7** beaded beads
- **8** 8mm round crystals
- **16** 3mm bicone crystals
- **16** 2mm round crystals
- Beading wire, .014
- Clasp
- 2 crimp beads
- Crimping pliers
- Wire cutters

1 On 1 yd. (.9m) of Fireline, center a pattern of a 10º cylinder bead and an 11º seed bead four times. Sew back through the first 10º picked up, and then retrace the thread path, skipping the 11ºs and pulling the beads into a square shape. Exit the first 10º **[fig. 1]**.

2 Pick up a 2mm round crystal and sew through the opposite 10º and the following 11º **[fig. 2]**.

3 Pick up a pattern of a 10º and an 11º three times, and then pick up a 10º. Sew through the 11º your thread exited at the start of this step. Retrace the thread path, skipping the 11ºs. Exit the 10º next to the 11º in the previous step, and then repeat step 2 **[fig. 3]**.

4 Repeat step 3 two more times.

5 Pick up a 10º, an 11º, and a 10º, and sew through the end 11º in the first unit. Pick up a 10º, an 11º, and a 10º, and sew through the 11º in the last unit. Retrace the thread path, skipping the 11ºs **[fig. 4]**. Repeat step 2.

6 Exit an 11º on the top or bottom of the ring of the beadwork. Pick up a 3mm bicone crystal, and sew through the next 11º in the ring. Repeat until you have five 3mms **[fig. 5]**. Reinforce the

ring of the 3mms with a second thread path, and exit a 3mm.

7 Pick up a 15º seed bead and sew through the next 3mm in the ring. Repeat around the ring, and step up through the first 15º added **[fig. 6]**.

8 Work a second round of 15ºs off the first round of 15ºs **[fig. 7]**, retrace the thread path to reinforce, and end the working thread.

9 Thread a needle on the tail, repeat steps 6–8 on the other side of the ring, and end the thread.

To make a bracelet
Cut 12 in. (30cm) of beading wire. Crimp half of the clasp on one end, and trim the excess. String a 3mm bicone, a 2mm, an 8mm, a 2mm, a 3mm, and a beaded bead. Repeat this pattern until you reach the desired length. Crimp the other half of the clasp on the other end, and trim the excess wire.

To make earrings
String a 3mm bicone crystal, a beaded bead, and a 3mm on a headpin. Make a wrapped loop, and attach it to an earring finding. Make a second earring.

Playtime

Bump up the sizes:
Use 8º seed beads and cylinders in place of 10º cylinders and 11º seed beads, and 11ºs instead of 15ºs. Use 3mm round crystals in place of 2mms, and 4mm bicones in place of 3mms.

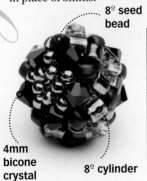

8º seed bead

4mm bicone crystal

8º cylinder

COLORS
- 4mm bicone crystals (Swarovski, garnet)
- 3mm round crystals (Swarovski, olivine)
- 8º cylinder beads (lined olive)
- 8º seed beads (matte dark olive)
- 11º seed beads (transparent light green luster)

Tiny Treasures

Modified netting encloses crystals in rings, making interesting little baubles. Strung on memory wire, they are focal beads as well as functional little covers for the ends of the memory wire. Make just two for earrings, shown on p. 29.

MATERIALS

For one bead 10mm

- **4** 4mm bicone crystals (Swarovski, white opal)
- **12** 11º seed beads (transparent blue)
- **48** 15º seed beads (transparent gray AB)
- Fireline 6 lb. test
- Beading needles, #12

Bracelet

- **10** beaded beads
- **18** 6mm bicone crystals (Swarovski, light sapphire satin)
- **18** 4mm bicone crystals (Swarovski, white opal)
- **18** 3mm bicone crystals (Swarovski, Montana)
- **63** 11º seed beads (transparent blue)
- Memory wire
- Memory wire cutters

Earrings

- **2** beaded beads (substitute colors listed below)
- **2** 4mm bicone crystals (Swarovski, cyclamen opal)
- **4** 3mm bicone crystals (Swarovski, light azore)
- **8** 11º seed beads (metallic blue)
- **2** headpins
- **2** earring findings
- Chainnose pliers
- Roundnose pliers
- Wire cutters

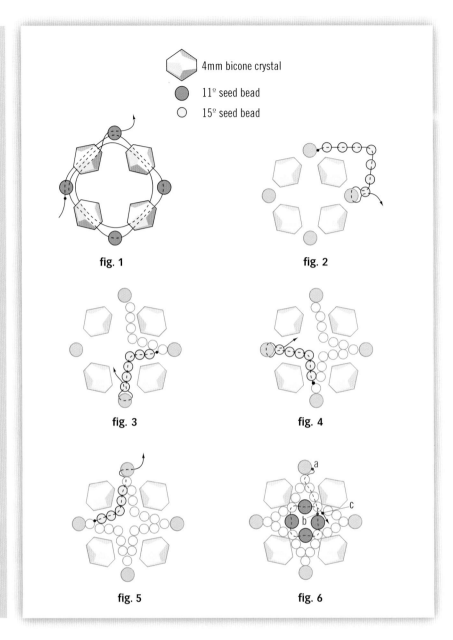

1 On 1 yd. (.9m) of Fireline, center a pattern of an 11º seed bead and a 4mm bicone crystal four times. Sew through the first 11º again to form a ring. Retrace the thread path, skipping the 11ºs, pulling the ring into a diamond shape. Exit an 11º **[fig. 1]**.

2 Pick up seven 15º seed beads, and sew through the next 11º in the ring and back through the last 15º picked up **[fig. 2]**.

3 Pick up six 15ºs, and sew through the next 11º in the ring and back through the last 15º picked up **[fig. 3]**.

4 Pick up six 15ºs, and sew through the next 11º in the ring and back through the last 15º picked up **[fig. 4]**.

5 Pick up five 15ºs, sew through the first 15º picked up in step 2, and then sew through the adjacent 11º **[fig. 5]**.

6 Sew through the first four 15ºs picked up in step 2 **[fig. 6, a–b]**. Pick up an 11º, and sew through the center 15º in the next stitch. Repeat this step three more times to close this end of the bead **[b–c]**. Retrace the new end ring of 11ºs, and end this thread.

7 Using the tail, repeat steps 2–6 on the other side of the initial ring.

To make a bracelet

Cut several coils of memory wire, and use 3–6mm bicone crystals and 11º seed beads to space the beaded beads. To finish the ends, make the first half of a beaded bead, string it on the end of the coil, and make a small loop or coil at the end of the wire. Complete the other half of the beaded bead to hide the loop of wire at the end.

To make earrings

String a beaded bead and 3mm bicone crystals and a 4mm bicone crystal separated by 11º seed beads on a headpin. Make a loop, and attach an earring finding.

COLORS

Large bead
- 6mm pearls (Swarovski, Tahitian look)
- 8º seed beads (matte teal)
- 11º seed beads (lined-gold AB)

Spike bead
- 6mm top-drilled crystals (Swarovski, greige)
- 11º seed beads (black)
- 15º seed beads (nickel-plated)

Small bead
- 4mm pearl (Swarovski, Tahitian look)
- 11º seed beads (metallic green)
- 15º seed beads (opal-lined)

Use 6mm top-drilled bicone crystals or 4mm round pearls in place of the 4mm crystals in the initial ring. Or, create a bigger bead using larger (6mm) pearls and substituting 8ºs for the 11ºs and 11ºs for the 15ºs.

8º seed bead

11º seed bead

6mm pearl

6mm top-drilled bicone

4mm pearl

Shooting Stars

Your color choice for the 3mm bicone crystals will determine how brightly your stars shine in these bold beaded beads. They are hollow; if desired, work around a lightweight bead or ball about 20mm in diameter to maintain the shape.

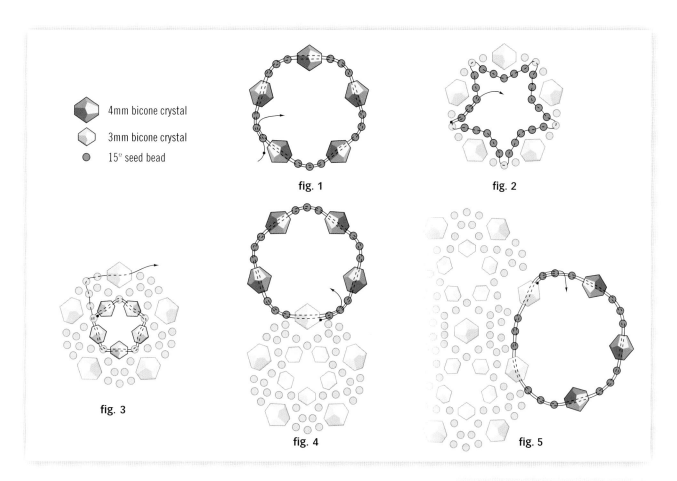

Key

- 4mm bicone crystal
- 3mm bicone crystal
- 15º seed bead

fig. 1

fig. 2

fig. 3

fig. 4

fig. 5

1 On 3 yd. (2.7m) of Fireline, pick up a pattern of three 15º seed beads and a 4mm bicone crystal five times. Sew through all the beads again to create a ring, leaving an 8-in. (20cm) tail. Sew through all the beads again to reinforce the ring, and exit a center 15º **[fig. 1]**.

2 Pick up five 15ºs, and sew through the next center 15º. Repeat to complete the round, and then step up through the first three 15ºs in the first set of five **[fig. 2]**.

3 Pick up a 3mm bicone crystal, and sew through the center 15º in the next set of five. Repeat around, and then reinforce the 3mms with a second thread path. Sew through the 15ºs to exit a 4mm along the outer ring **[fig. 3]**.

4 On each 4mm of the original ring, you will add new rings. Some of the 4mms will be shared. Pick up a repeating pattern of three 15ºs and a 4mm four times, and then

pick up three 15ºs. Sew through the 4mm in the previous ring. Reinforce all the beads in the new ring, and exit a center 15º **[fig. 4]**. Repeat step 2 and 3 to add the 15º netting and 3mms. Exit a side 4mm next to the connecting 4mm.

5 Connect a new 4mm ring to the two previous rings: Pick up a pattern of three 15ºs and a 4mm three times, then pick up three 15ºs. Sew through the next outer 4mm on the first ring. Pick up three 15ºs, and sew through the 4mm your thread exited at the start of this step. Reinforce all the beads in the new ring, exiting a center 15º **[fig. 5]**, and then repeat steps 2 and 3.

6 Pick up three 15ºs, and sew through the next 4mm on the original ring. Pick up a pattern of three 15ºs and a 4mm three times, then pick up three 15ºs. Sew through the 4mm your thread exited at the start of this step, and then reinforce all the beads in the new ring, exiting a center 15º. Repeat

MATERIALS
Green bead 25mm
- **60** 4mm bicone crystals (Swarovski, jet AB 2X)
- **60** 3mm bicone crystals (Swarovski, light azore)
- 3 grams 15º seed beads (silver-lined teal)
- 20mm lightweight bead or other form (optional)
- Fireline 6 lb. test
- Beading needles, #12 or #13

Rose bead
- 4mm bicone crystals (Swarovski, light rose champagne)
- 3mm bicone crystals (Swarovski, sand opal)
- 15º seed beads (transparent raspberry)

Purple bead
- 4mm bicone crystals (Swarovski, purple velvet)
- 3mm bicone crystals (Swarovski, ruby)
- 15º seed beads (metallic blue)

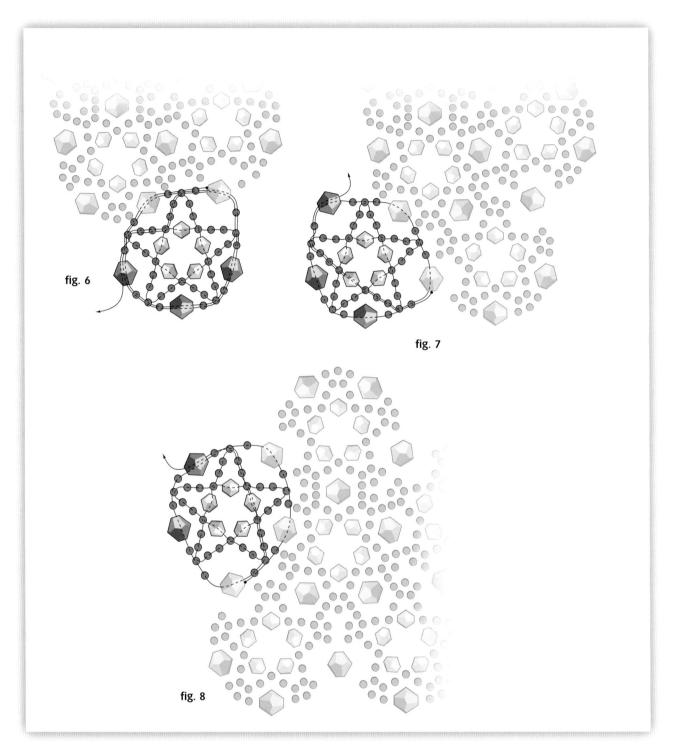

fig. 6

fig. 7

fig. 8

steps 2 and 3, and then exit a side 4mm in the new ring **[fig. 6]**.

7 Pick up a pattern of three 15ºs and a 4mm three times, and then pick up three 15ºs. Sew through the next 4mm on the original ring. Pick up three 15ºs, and sew through the 4mm your thread exited at the start of this step. Reinforce all the beads in the new ring, exiting a center 15º. Repeat steps 2 and 3, and then exit a side 4mm in the new ring **[fig. 7]**.

8 Pick up three 15ºs, and sew through the next 4mm in the original ring. Pick up three 15ºs, and sew through the side 4mm of the second ring. Pick up a repeating pattern of three 15ºs and a 4mm two times, and then pick up three 15ºs. Sew through the 4mm your thread exited at the start of this step, and reinforce all the beads in the ring, exiting a center 15º. Repeat steps 2 and 3, and exit a 4mm in the new ring **[fig. 8]**.

This completes the first half of the bead. If desired, insert a form to shape the second half around.

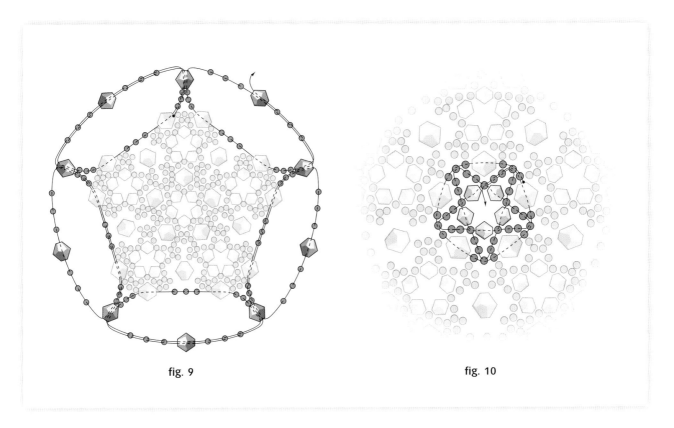

fig. 9

fig. 10

9 Work the second half of the bead off the 4mms along the outer edge of the first half. Make five more rings with five crystals in each ring **[fig. 9]**. Complete each ring before moving on to the next one (not shown).

10 The last ring will be formed by working off the 4mms from each of the five rings just completed. Exit one of these open 4mms, pick up three 15ºs, and sew through the next open 4mm added in the previous step. Repeat to close up the last ring, and finish as in steps 2 and 3 **[fig. 10]**. End the threads.

To create a spiky version of this beaded bead, substitute teardrop pendant beads in place of the 4mm crystals.

teardrop pendant crystal

COLORS
- 11mm teardrop pendant crystals (Swarovski, crystal AB)
- 3mm bicone crystals (Swarovski, tanzanite)
- 15º seed beads (matte purple/blue)

Component
Craze

Butterflies Abound

These beautiful crystal butterflies can dance on your wrist or flutter near your ears.

MATERIALS
One butterfly (green)
- **31** 3mm bicone crystals (Swarovski, jet AB 2X)
- 1–2 grams 15º seed beads (gold-lined teal)
- Fireline 6 lb. test
- Beading needles, #12 or #13

Bracelet
- **6** butterflies
- **186** 3mm bicone crystals (Swarovski, jet AB 2X)
- 4–5 grams 15º seed beads (gold-lined teal)
- Clasp
- **2** 3mm jump rings

Amethyst butterfly
- 3mm bicone crystals (Swarovski, amethyst)
- 15º seed beads (gunmetal)

Brown butterfly
- 3mm bicone crystals (Swarovski, Colorado topaz)
- 15º seed beads (metallic bronze)

1 On 1 yd. (.9m) of Fireline, center a 3mm bicone crystal and eight 15º seed beads. Holding the beads in place, skip the last 15º, and sew back through the next 15º **[fig. 1]**.

2 Pick up six 15ºs, and sew through the 3mm picked up in step 1 **[fig. 2]**. This completes the shape of the body.

3 Pick up four 15ºs, skip the 15º just picked up, and sew back through the next three 15ºs, the 3mm, and the next 15º **[fig. 3]**.

4 Pick up five 3mms and a 15º. Skip the last 15º, and sew back through the 3mm to form the top of the first wing **[fig. 4]**.

5 Pick up four 3mms, and sew through the fourth 15º on the same side of the body and back through the last 3mm picked up **[fig. 5]**.

6 Pick up three 3mms and a 15º, skip the 15º, and sew back through the last 3mm **[fig. 6]**.

7 Pick up three 3mms, and sew through the sixth 15º on the same side of the body. Sew back through the beads in both wings, retracing the thread path **[fig. 7]**. Secure the thread in the 15ºs on this side of the body, but don't end the thread if you plan to connect the butterflies.

8 Using the other thread, repeat steps 3–7 on the second side of the body **[fig. 8]**.

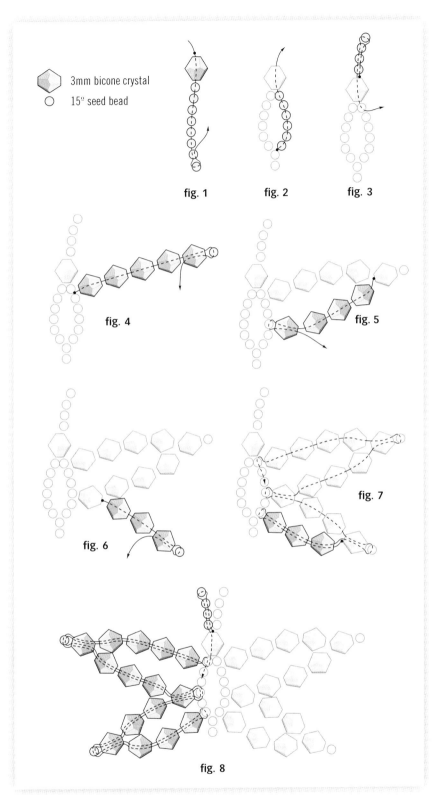

○ 3mm bicone crystal
○ 15º seed bead

fig. 1   fig. 2   fig. 3

fig. 4   fig. 5

fig. 6   fig. 7

fig. 8

To connect butterflies into a bracelet

Work steps 1–8 for the first butterfly. For the second and all subsequent butterflies, repeat steps 1–7. Repeat step 8, but in the second repeat of steps 4 and 6, sew through the 15º from the bottom wing and top wing, respectively, of the previous butterfly. Every other butterfly will be upside down **[fig. 9]**. Make and connect the number of butterflies to achieve the desired length. Make a loop of 11º seed beads connecting the end 15ºs of the end butterflies. End the threads. Open a jump ring, and attach half of the clasp to the 15ºs in the wings of each end butterfly.

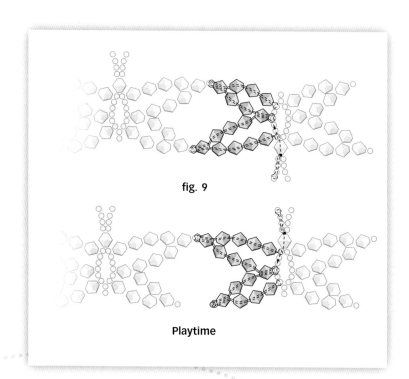

fig. 9

Playtime

This memory-wire necklace uses the same colors as in the bracelet, but I used 4mms for two butterflies and 5mms for the center butterfly. You'll need about 90 additional 4mm bicone crystals and a few grams of 11º seed beads to string between them.

Work steps 1–8 for the first butterfly. For the second and third butterflies, repeat steps 1–7. Repeat step 8, but in the second repeat of step 4, pick up the 11º from the top wing of the previous butterfly **[figure]**. Cut an overlapping coil of necklace-size memory wire. Make a plain loop at one end, and pick up a pattern of a 4mm bicone and an 11º 33 times. Slide the 11º on the left side of the end antenna onto the memory wire. Pick up a crystal, and then pick up the 11º on the right side of the end antenna. Pick up a pattern of a 3mm and an 11º six times, and then pick up a 4mm. Repeat to connect the remaining butterflies. Stitch the tips of the end wings to an 11º on the memory wire.

Playtime

Northern Lights Necklace

Capture a rivoli with netting and
herringbone stitch, and then add
sparkling crystal-topped spikes.

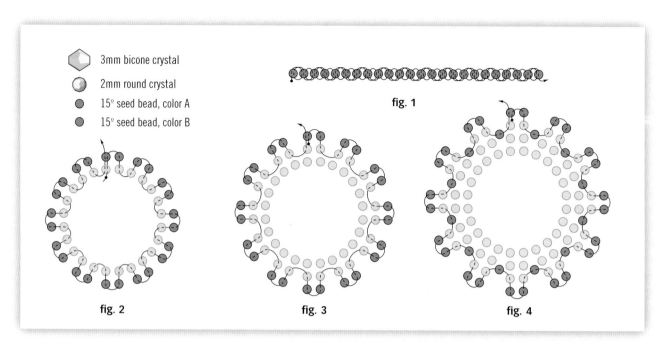

Legend:
- 3mm bicone crystal
- 2mm round crystal
- 15º seed bead, color A
- 15º seed bead, color B

fig. 1

fig. 2

fig. 3

fig. 4

MATERIALS

One component 29mm
- 14mm rivoli (Swarovski, purple haze)
- **12** 3mm bicone crystals (Swarovski, cyclamen opal)
- **12** 2mm round crystals (Swarovski, amethyst)
- 3 grams 15º seed beads, color A (metallic olive)
- 2 grams 15º seed beads, color B (transparent light purple)
- 3–4mm soldered jump ring
- Fireline 4 or 6 lb. test
- Beading needles, #12 or #13

Necklace 18 in. (46cm)
- Component
- **7** 8mm rondelle crystals (Swarovski, **5** purple haze, **2** khaki)
- **17** 6mm bicone crystals (Swarovski, light amethyst)
- **21** 4mm bicone crystals (Swarovski, khaki)
- **24** 3mm bicone crystals (Swarovski, amethyst AB)
- **26** 2mm round crystals (Swarovski, amethyst)
- 3 grams 11º seed beads (metallic olive)
- Clasp
- 1½ in. (3.8cm) of chain for extender
- **4** 22-gauge headpins

1 On 2 yd. (1.8m) of Fireline, pick up two color-A 15º seed beads, leaving a 20-in. (51cm) tail. Sew back through both As again, and position them next to each other so the holes are parallel. Continue in ladder stitch, picking up an A, and sew through the previous A and the new A until you have 24 As **[fig. 1]**. Sew up through the first A, sew down through the last A, and then sew up through the first A again to form a ring.

2 Working in herringbone stitch, pick up two As, sew down through the next A in the ring, and sew up through the following A in the ring. Repeat this step around the ring, and step up through the first A added in this round **[fig. 2]**.

3 Work a second round of herringbone: Pick up two As, sew down through the next A in the previous round, and sew up through the following A. Repeat this step to complete the round, and step up through the first A added in this round **[fig. 3]**.

4 Work an increase round: Pick up two As, sew down through the next A, pick up a color-B 15º, and sew up through the following A in the previous round. Repeat these two stitches to complete the round, and step up through the first A added in this round **[fig. 4]**.

5 To make the spikes: Pick up an A, a 3mm bicone crystal, and an A. Sew back through

the 3mm, pick up an A, sew down through the next two As and the B, and sew up through the following two As **[fig. 5, a–b]**. Repeat once **[b–c]**. On the third spike, pick up an A, a 3mm, an A, and the jump ring. Sew back through the A and the 3mm, and pick up an A. Sew down through the next two As and the B, and sew up through the following two As **[c–d]**. Work the next two spikes as the first two. For the next two spikes, work as before, but pick up two As, a 3mm, and an A. Sew back through the 3mm, pick up two As, sew down through the next two As and the B, and sew up through the next two As. For the next spike, pick up three As to start, and four for the next. Pick up three As for the next spike, and then for the next two spikes, pick up two As **[d–e]**. Set aside the working thread.

6 Using the tail, pick up five As, skip two As in the initial ring, sew down through the next A, and sew up through the following A. Repeat this step around the ring. Step up through the first three As added in this step **[fig. 6, a–b]**.

7 Pick up three As, and sew through the center A in the next stitch of five. Repeat around, and step up through the first two As added in the first stitch of this step **[b–c]**.

8 Pick up a B, and sew through the center A in the next stitch. Repeat around **[c–d]**, and sew through the six beads that make up the

fig. 5

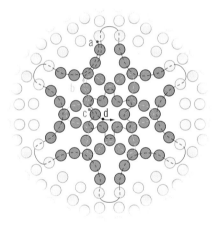

fig. 6

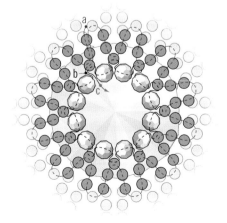

fig. 7

center ring several times to reinforce. End the tail.

9 With the working thread, make sure you are exiting a B between two spikes. Pick up five Bs, and sew through the next B in the same round. (Check to make sure the 15ºs cover the edge of the rivoli when placed in the center of the pendant; you may have to use seven Bs instead of five.) Repeat around the ring, and step up through the first three Bs in the first stitch [fig. 7, a–b].

10 Place the rivoli in the center of the netted stitches from step 9. Holding the rivoli in place, pick up a 2mm round crystal, and sew through the center B in the next

stitch. Repeat to complete the round [b–c], and then sew through the 2mms and Bs that make up the center ring to reinforce. End the thread.

11 For stringing, use a purchased cord, or crimp a clasp on one end of a piece of beading wire. String a pleasing arrangement of crystals and 15ºs to the center of the desired length, string the pendant, and then string the second half of the necklace to match the first half. Crimp a clasp on one end, and trim the ends.

12 On the other end, crimp a length of chain, and embellish the chain with crystal dangles. (See p. 79 for extender ideas.)

COLORS
Black/gold pendant
- 14mm rivoli (Swarovski, purple haze)
- 3mm bicone crystals (Swarovski, crystal metallic light gold)
- 2mm round crystals (Swarovski, jet)
- 15º seed beads:
  Color A (gold iris)
  Color B (black)

Purple/blue pendant
- 14mm rivoli (Swarovski, light vitrail)
- 4mm and 3mm bicone crystals

(Swarovski, light amethyst)
- 2mm round crystals (Swarovski, crystal)
- 15º seed beads (matte purple/blue)

Purple pendant
- 14mm rivoli (Swarovski, light vitrail)
- 3mm bicone crystals (Swarovski, cyclamen opal)
- 2mm round crystals (Swarovski, amethyst)
- 15º seed beads:
  Color A (transparent amethyst)
  Color B (purple iris)

Vary your color palette or use Northern Lights components to make a fun bracelet or a ring.

Moons of Jupiter Bracelet

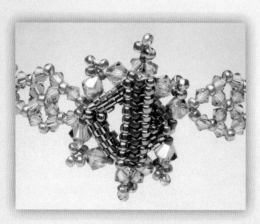

Capture pearls in lovely layers of seed beads and crystals. Clasp the bracelet with a herringbone toggle bar through a peyote stitch ring.

MATERIALS
Bracelet 7 in. (18cm)
- **7** 8mm pearls (Swarovski, white)
- Bicone crystals:
  64 4mm to embellish the
  components and clasp (Swarovski,
  tanzanite AB 2X)
  96 3mm to connect 7 components
  (Swarovski, tanzanite)
- 3–4 grams 11º seed beads
  (transparent teal AB)
- 3 grams 15º cylinder beads (matte
  silver)
- 2 grams 15º seed beads (matte
  teal green)
- ½ in. (1.3cm) small-link chain
- Fireline 6 lb. test
- Beading needles, #12 and #13

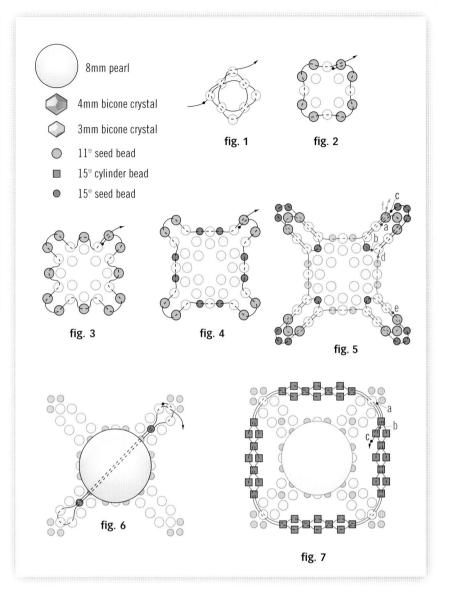

fig. 1

fig. 2

fig. 3

fig. 4

fig. 5

fig. 6

fig. 7

1 On 2 yd. (1.8m) of Fireline, pick up eight 11º seed beads. Sew through the first bead again to form a ring, leaving a 24-in. (61cm) tail. Sew through every other 11º in the ring to form a square, exiting a corner bead [**fig. 1**]. Finesse the beads a bit if necessary to shape the square.

2 Work a round of herringbone by picking up two 11ºs and sewing through the next corner bead. Repeat this step three times, and then step up through the first 11º added in this step [**fig. 2**].

3 Alternate a herringbone stitch and a peyote stitch by picking up two 11ºs and sewing down through the next 11º in the previous round. Pick up an 11º, and sew up through the next 11º in the previous round. Repeat these two stitches three times, and step up [**fig. 3**].

4 Alternate a herringbone stitch and two peyote stitches by picking up two 11ºs and sewing down through the next 11º in the previous round. Pick up a 15º seed bead, and sew through the next 11º in the previous round. Pick up a 15º, and sew through the next 11º. Repeat these three stitches three times, and step up through the first 11º in the new round [**fig. 4**].

5 Pick up three 11ºs, and sew down through the next two 11ºs in the stack [**fig. 5, a–b**]. Pick up a 15º, and sew up through three 11ºs in the adjacent column [**b–c**], adding the 15º to the outside spoke. Pick up three 15ºs, and sew down through three 11ºs in the column [**c–d**], positioning them to the outside of the center 11º on the spoke. Sew though the next 15º, 11º, 15º, and two 11ºs in the next spoke [**d–e**]. Repeat this step three times, and exit the first 11º added in the first spoke [**e–f**].

6 Sew through the center 11º and down through the next 11º in the stack. Pick up a 15º, a 8mm pearl, and a 15º. Sew up through the top 11º and the center 11º, and sew down through the next 11º in the opposite stack. Sew back through the 15º, the pearl, and the 15º. Sew up through the opposite column [**fig. 6**]. This will pull the two spokes together; don't pull the thread too tight or the component will be lopsided.

7 Pick up seven 15º cylinder beads, and sew through the center 11º on the next spoke. Repeat this stitch three times, and step up through the first cylinder in this round [**fig. 7, a–b**].

8 Work a round of peyote using cylinders: Pick up a cylinder, skip a cylinder in the ring, and sew through the next cylinder. Work two more stitches, then sew through the next center 11º and following cylinder. Repeat these stitches three times, and step up through the first two cylinders [**b–c**].

9 Work two stitches using cylinders, pick up an 11º, and sew through the second cylinder in the next set of stitches close to the pearl to form a square. Repeat these stitches three times [**fig. 8**], and end the working thread.

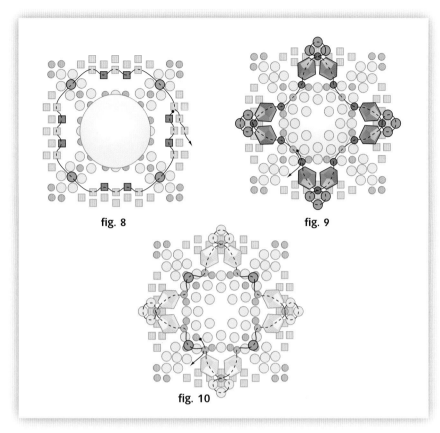

fig. 8

fig. 9

fig. 10

10 Using the tail on the bottom, sew through an 11º in the column, and exit the 15º added in step 5. Pick up a 15º, a 4mm bicone crystal, a 15º, and three 11ºs. Skip the last three 11ºs, and sew back through the 15º to form a picot. Pick up a 4mm and a 15º, and sew through the 15º in the next column. Repeat this step three times [**fig. 9**].

11 Retrace the thread path to reinforce the crystals, and add an 11º between the 15ºs at the end and beginning of each stitch added in step 9 [**fig. 10**]. End the tail. Make five pearl components.

12 To connect components: Attach a stop bead to the end of 1 yd. (.9m) of thread, leaving a 6-in. (15cm) tail. Sew through one of the 11ºs added in step 11. Pick up a pattern of an 11º and a 3mm bicone crystal four times, and then pick up an 11º. Sew through the corresponding 11º added in step 11 on another component. Pick up a pattern of an 11º and a 3mm four times, then pick up an 11º. Sew through the 11º on the first component to create a ring [**fig. 11, a–b**].

13 Sew through the first 11º, 3mm, and 11º in the ring [**b–c**]. Pick up a 3mm, 11º, and 3mm,

skip a 3mm, 11º, and 3mm in the ring, and sew through the next 11º, 3mm, three 11ºs, 3mm, and 11º [**c–d**]. Pick up a 3mm, and sew through the 11º just added [**d–e**]. Pick up a 3mm. Skip the next 3mm, 11º, and 3mm in the ring, and sew through the next 11º, 3mm, and 11º [**e–f**]. Reinforce the thread path, remove the stop bead, and end the threads.

Toggle clasp

14 On 1 yd. (.9m) of thread, pick up a pattern of an 11º and seven 15º cylinder beads four times, leaving a 6-in. (15cm) tail. Sew through the first 11º to form a ring, and then sew through the next cylinder. Work three peyote stitches using cylinders, and then sew through the next 11º and cylinder. Repeat these stitches three times, and step up through the first two cylinders [**fig. 12**].

15 Work two stitches using cylinders and one stitch using an 11º, pulling the ring into a square. Repeat these stitches three times, and exit an outer 11º [**fig. 13**]. Pick up an 11º, sew through the 11º in the outer ring again, and then sew through the new 11º.

16 Work as in steps 14 and 15 to create a second ring [**fig. 14**], working off the 11ºs

added in step 14 instead of picking up new 11ºs. Work an extra round of peyote using two cylinders per side around the outside of the ring. Fold the two rings together, and zip up the outer rounds of peyote, exiting a corner 11º.

17 Pick up a 15º seed bead, a 4mm, a 15º, and three 11ºs. Sew through the 15º again to make a picot, and then pick up a 4mm and a 15º. Sew through the next 11º in the ring. Repeat this step three times [**fig. 15**]. Sew through the beadwork to exit a corner 11º on the other surface of the ring. Reinforce the beads and crystals added in this step, sewing through the corner 11ºs on the other side of the ring.

18 Attach the toggle ring to an end component as in steps 13 and 14, and end the threads.

19 Thread a needle on each end of 1½ yd. (.9m) of thread, and center an 11º. Pick up a 15º seed bead on one needle and cross the other needle through it so the holes are parallel. Repeat with an 11º and 15º seed bead. Cross the needles through the first 11º to form a small ring [**fig. 16**].

20 With one needle, working in herringbone stitch, pick up an 11º and a 15º. Sew down through the next 15º, and sew up through the following 11º in the ring. Repeat the last stitch, but step up through the first 11º added [**fig. 17**]. Repeat until you have 11 rounds of herringbone. Work a thread path to close up the last round to mimic the first, and end the working thread.

21 With the remaining needle, pick up a 15º, a 3mm crystal, a 15º, and three 11ºs. Skip the 11ºs, and sew back through the 15º to form a picot. Pick up a 3mm and a 15º, and sew into the opposite column of 11ºs on this end. Sew through all the 11ºs in this column to exit the other end. Repeat this embellishment on the other end, and then sew through the beadwork to exit a center 15º [**fig. 18**]. Stitch through an end link of the chain and back through the 15º. Retrace the thread path several times, and end the thread.

22 Open a jump ring, and attach the toggle bar to the remaining end component as in steps 13 and 14, but sew through the end link in the chain instead of an 11º.

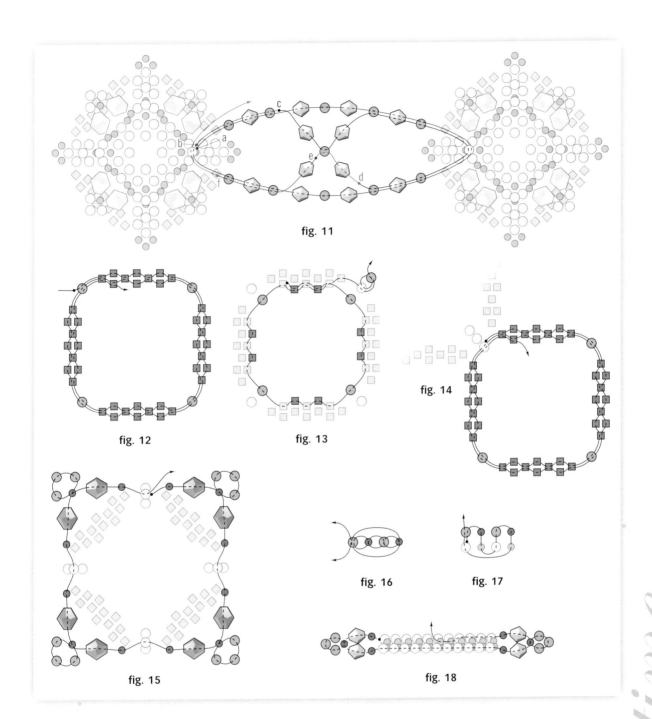

fig. 11

fig. 12

fig. 13

fig. 14

fig. 15

fig. 16

fig. 17

fig. 18

A single moon component makes a cool ring top.
Add a ladder stitch band of 11° seed beads.

**11° seed
bead**

COLORS
- 8mm pearl (Swarovski, black)
- 4mm bicone crystals (Swarovski, tanzanite AB 2X)
- 11° seed beads (light gray AB)
- 15° seed beads (metallic blue)
- 15° cylinder beads (transparent amethyst)

Playtime

Surround a rivoli or other fancy stone with an unusual bugle-bead bezel of right-angle weave to create a stunning pendant.

Architectural Appeal Pendant

1 On 2 yd. (1.8m) of Fireline, pick up a repeating pattern of an 11º seed bead and a 6mm bugle bead four times. Sew through all the beads again to form a ring, leaving a 6-in. (15cm) tail. Retrace the thread path, skipping the 11ºs to form a tight square. Exit an 11º **[fig. 1]**.

2 Pick up a pattern of a color-A 4mm bicone crystal and an 11º three times. Pick up an A, and sew back through the 11º your thread exited at the start of this step. Retrace the thread path, skipping the 11ºs. Sew through the beadwork to exit the next corner 11º in the square. Repeat on all corners **[fig. 2]**.

3 Place the rivoli with the front facing the bugle beads. Wrap the crystal corners around it to see how much space is between the 11ºs and the crystal points. This space will be filled in later with the small bugle beads and 15ºs as needed, after closing up the back of the pendant. Sew through to an opposite 11º from one of the corner 11ºs in the bugle square **[fig. 3]**.

4 Working on the back of the rivoli, pick up a 6mm bugle bead, and sew through the corresponding 11º in the next crystal corner. Repeat three more times, adding a 15º before and after each bugle bead if your focal bead is too big for the structure, and then retrace the thread path, skipping the 11ºs to form a tight square **[fig. 4]**. Sew through the beadwork to exit one of the 11ºs along the outer edge between two crystals.

5 Pick up a 15º seed bead, a 3mm bugle, and a 15º, and sew though the next 11º along the outer edge. Pick up a 15º, a 3mm bugle bead, and a 15º, and sew through the 11º your thread exited at the start of this step **[fig. 5]**. Sew though the next A 4mm, 11º, A 4mm, and 11º to add the 15ºs and 3mm bugle beads between the remaining three sets of outer edge 11ºs.

MATERIALS
Pendant 1 in. (2.5cm)
- 16mm rivoli (Swarovski, purple haze)
- **16** 4mm bicone crystals, color A (Swarovski, crystal celadon)
- **8** 4mm bicone crystals, color B (Swarovski, white opal celadon)
- **8** 6mm bugle beads for the front of the pendant (purple iris)
- **8** 3mm bugle beads for the outer edge (matte dark olive)
- 1–2 grams 11º seed beads (matte dark purple)
- 1–2 grams 15º seed beads (dark olive)
- 4–6mm jump ring
- Necklace chain or cord
- Fireline 6 lb. test
- Beading needles, #12 or #13

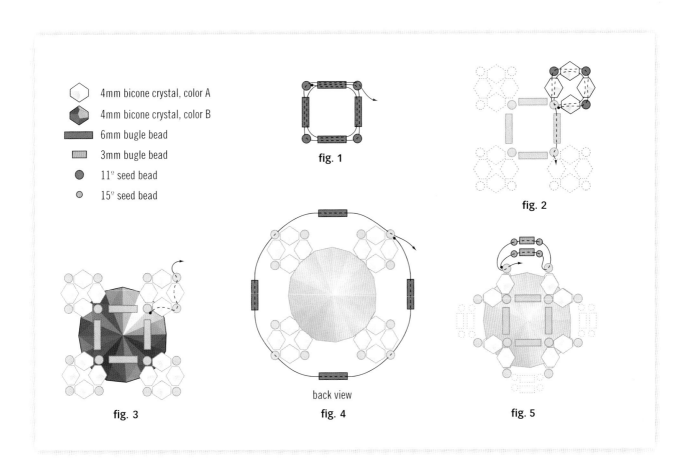

4mm bicone crystal, color A
4mm bicone crystal, color B
6mm bugle bead
3mm bugle bead
11º seed bead
15º seed bead

fig. 1

fig. 2

fig. 3

back view
fig. 4

fig. 5

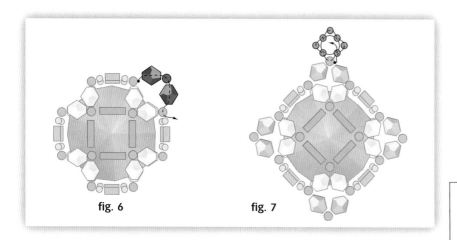

fig. 6   fig. 7

6 Add points to the crystal corners by exiting an 11º along the outer edge. Pick up a color-B 4mm bicone crystal, an 11º, and a B, and sew through the next 11º along the outer edge **[fig. 6]**. Sew back though the last B, 11º, and first B just picked up. Sew through the 11º your thread exited at the

start of this step. Repeat on all four crystal corners. Exit an 11º between two Bs.

7 Pick up seven 15ºs, and sew though the 11º your thread exited at the start of this step. Retrace the thread path, skipping the corner 15ºs to create a diamond shape **[fig. 7]**. End the threads.

Playtime

Use other sizes of crystal fancy stones in the center of the bugle bead cage. Or, to create an elongated diamond shape, add a point only to opposite crystal corners in step 6. To make a ring, attach a ladder stitch band to the opposite bugle beads.

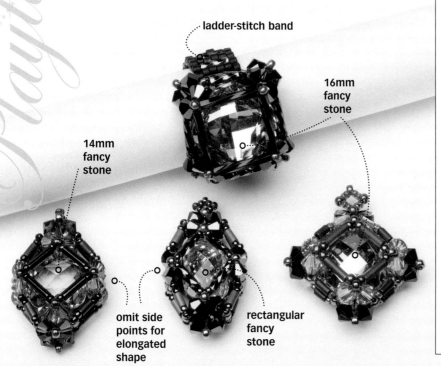

ladder-stitch band

16mm fancy stone

14mm fancy stone

omit side points for elongated shape

rectangular fancy stone

COLORS
Ring
- 16mm checkerboard fancy stone (Swarovski, crystal silver shade)
- 4mm bicone crystals (Swarovski, jet hematite 2X)
- 12mm bugle beads (black)
- 6mm twisted bugle beads (gunmetal)
- 11º seed beads (nickel-plated)

Blue/purple pendant
- 14mm checkerboard fancy stone (Swarovski, Indian sapphire)
- 4mm bicone crystals:
  Color A (Swarovski, tanzanite)
  Color B (Swarovski, Montana)
- 6mm bugle beads (purple iris)
- 3mm bugle beads (matte purple iris)
- 11º seed beads (transparent amethyst AB)
- 15º seed beads (metallic blue)

Silver pendant
- Rectangular fancy stone (Swarovski, crystal silver-lined foiled)
- 4mm bicone crystals (Swarovski, jet hematite 2X)
- 6mm twisted bugle beads (gunmetal)
- 3mm bugle beads (matte silver)
- 11º seed beads (nickel-plated)
- 15º seed beads (gunmetal)

Brown pendant
- 16mm checkerboard fancy stone (Swarovski, crystal golden shadow)
- 4mm bicone crystals:
  Color A (Swarovski, crystal golden shadow)
  Color B (Swarovski, mocha)
- 6mm bugle beads (matte brown)
- 3mm bugle beads (matte purple iris)
- 11º seed beads (gold iris)
- 15º seed beads (gold iris)

Victorian Echoes Bracelet

This graceful bracelet uses a soft color palette and comfy pearls with crystal embellishments. Layers of seed beads add detail and give you the opportunity to play with accent color.

MATERIALS

Bracelet 7¾ in. (19.7cm)

- **48** 6mm round crystal pearls (Swarovski, soft green)
- **12** 5mm bicone crystals (Swarovski, purple velvet)
- 1–2 grams 11º seed beads (metallic green)
- 3–4 grams 15º seed beads (metallic green)
- Clasp
- **2** 3mm jump rings
- Fireline 4 or 6 lb. test
- Beading needles, #12 or #13

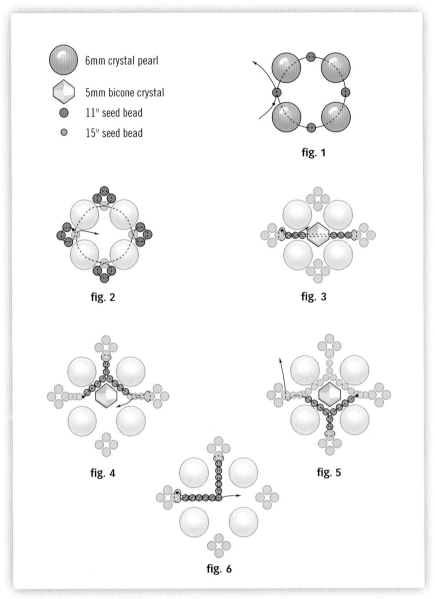

6mm crystal pearl

5mm bicone crystal

11º seed bead

15º seed bead

fig. 1

fig. 2

fig. 3

fig. 4

fig. 5

fig. 6

1 On a comfortable length of thread, pick up a pattern of an 11º seed bead and a 6mm pearl four times. Sew back through the first 11º again to form a ring [**fig. 1**], leaving a 12-in. (30cm) tail.

2 Pick up three 11ºs and sew back through the 11º your thread is exiting, the next 6mm, and the following 11º in the ring. Repeat three times [**fig. 2**].

3 Pick up three 15º seed beads, a 5mm bicone crystal, and three 15ºs. Sew through the opposite 11º in the ring and back through all the beads just picked up, the opposite 11º, and two new 15ºs [**fig. 3**].

4 Pick up six 15ºs, and sew through the next 11º in the ring and back through the last two 15ºs picked up. Pick up four 15ºs, and sew through the last two 15ºs from step 3, the adjacent 11º, and back through the last two 15ºs again [**fig. 4**].

5 Pick up six 15ºs, sew through the next 11º in the ring, and back through the last two 15ºs picked up. Pick up four 15ºs, and sew through the first two 15ºs from step 3 and the adjacent 11º, bringing the thread to the back of the component [**fig. 5**].

6 On the back of the component, pick up 11 15ºs, and sew through the next 11º in the ring. Sew back through all the 15ºs just added, the 11º your thread exited at the start of the step, and the first six 15ºs added in this step [**fig. 6**].

7 Pick up five 15ºs, and sew through the next open 11º in the ring. Sew back through the five 15ºs just added and the 15º your thread exited at the start of this step. Repeat this step to complete the X, and then sew through the beadwork to exit the 11º opposite the 11º the tail is exiting and the next two 11ºs [**fig. 7**].

8 Pick up a pattern of a 6mm and an 11º three times, and then pick up a 6mm. Sew through the 11º your thread exited at the start of this step and the next two beads [**fig. 8**]. Make the next component as in steps 2–7. Continue connecting components to the previous one until you reach the desired length.

9 To add the clasp, exit an end 11º as before, and pick up 11 15ºs. Sew back through the 11º, and then retrace the thread path, skipping every third 15º to pull the beads into a diamond shape [**fig. 9**]. End the thread, and repeat this step with the tail on the other end.

10 Open a jump ring, and attach half of the clasp to an end ring. Repeat on the other end.

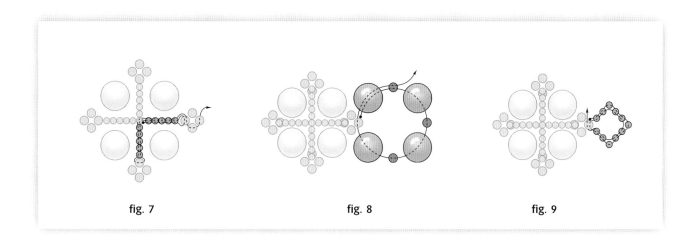

fig. 7   fig. 8   fig. 9

COLORS

Earrings

- 6mm helix crystals (Swarovski, crystal silver shade)
- 5mm bicone crystals (Swarovski, jet)
- 11º seed beads (matte black)
- 15º seed beads (matte nickel)

Bracelet

- 6mm helix crystals (Swarovski, crystal)
- 5mm bicone crystals (Swarovski, amethyst)
- 11º seed beads (transparent amethyst)
- 15º seed beads (transparent amethyst AB)

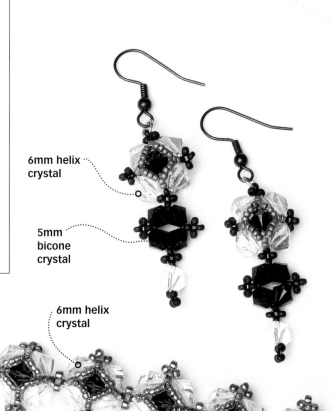

6mm helix crystal

5mm bicone crystal

6mm helix crystal

Use 6mm helix crystals in place of 6mm pearls to make sparkling versions of these components. For darling earring dangles, pair a component with a base ring of bicones.

Tulip Bracelet

Dainty components of modified herringbone stand up like fresh tulip blossoms in this delicate bracelet.

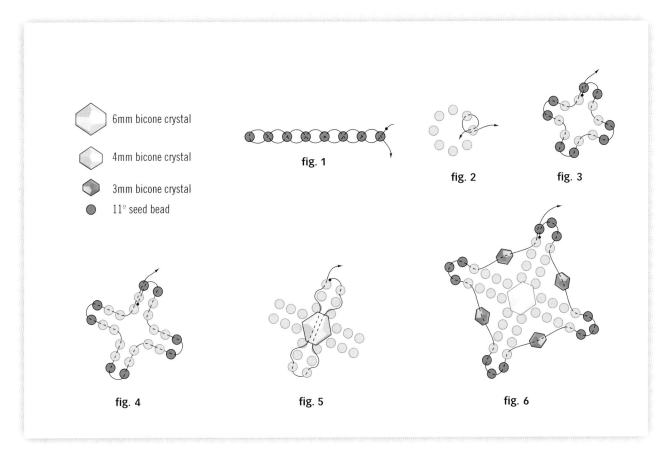

fig. 1

fig. 2

fig. 3

fig. 4

fig. 5

fig. 6

Legend:
- 6mm bicone crystal
- 4mm bicone crystal
- 3mm bicone crystal
- 11° seed bead

MATERIALS

Blue bracelet 7 in. (18cm)
- 8 6mm bicone crystals (Swarovski, light azore)
- **50** 4mm bicone crystals (Swarovski, tanzanite)
- **32** 3mm bicone crystals (Swarovski, light azore)
- 4 grams 11° seed beads (blue)
- Clasp
- **2** 6mm jump rings
- Fireline 6 lb. test
- Beading needles, #12

Purple bracelet
- 6mm bicone crystals (Swarovski, purple velvet)
- 4mm bicone crystals (Swarovski, violet)
- 3mm bicone crystals (Swarovski, tanzanite)
- 11° seed beads (matte blue iris)

1 Thread a needle on each end of 1 yd. (.9m) of Fireline. Make a ladder stitch strip of eight 11° seed beads: Pick up two 11°s, and bring the beads to about 8 in. (20cm) from one end of the thread. Cross the shorter tail through the second bead, making the holes sit parallel to each other. Pick up an 11° on one needle, and cross the other needle through it. Repeat until you have eight beads [**fig. 1**].

2 Cross both needles through the first 11° to create a ring [**fig. 2**]. Cross both needles through the next few beads to secure the join. You can remove the needle from the short tail if desired.

3 Work a round of tubular herringbone: Pick up two 11°s, sew down through the next 11° in the ring, and sew up through the following 11°. Repeat this step three times, but on the last repeat, step up through the first 11° added in the new round [**fig. 3**].

4 Work another round of tubular herringbone: Pick up two 11°s, sew down through the next two 11°s, and sew up through the following two 11°s in the next stack. Repeat to complete the round, but on the last repeat, step up through three 11°s instead of two [**fig. 4**].

5 Sew through the next 11°. Pick up a 6mm bicone crystal, sew up through the opposite 11°, and sew down through the next 11°. Sew back through the 6mm and up through the 11° your thread exited at the start of this step [**fig. 5**].

6 Work another round of tubular herringbone, sewing through all the beads in each stack.

7 Pick up three 11°s, and sew down through the next 11°. Pick up a 3mm bicone crystal, and sew up through the next 11°. Repeat three times, but on the last repeat, step up through the first 11° added in this step [**fig. 6**]. Retrace the thread path, and exit a bead in the ladder round.

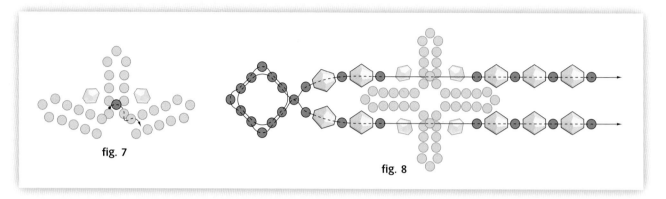

fig. 7

fig. 8

8 Sew through the ladder round so the thread is pointing up toward the top of the tulip in a stack between two 3mms. Pick up an 11º, and sew down through the next 11º in the ladder round and up through the next 11º [**fig. 7**]. Zigzag through the ladder round to exit the opposite stack, and add an 11º. Retrace the thread path, and end the threads.

9 Make eight tulips, being sure to add the two 11ºs in step 8 to the same stacks as the first tulip so the bicone crystals all face the same way when picked up.

10 Thread a needle on each end of 1 yd. (.9m) of Fireline, and center 12 11ºs. Cross one needle through the last 11º picked up, and then continue through all the beads, skipping every third bead to pull the beads into a diamond shape. Exit so the two threads are exiting opposite ends of the same bead.

11 On each needle, pick up an 11º, a 4mm bicone crystal, an 11º, a 4mm, and an 11º.

12 With each needle, sew through the side 11º on the tulip added in step 8. Pick up a pattern of an 11º and a 4mm three times,

and then pick up an 11º [**fig. 8**]. Repeat this step to pick up all the tulips. End with an 11º, a 4mm, an 11º, a 4mm, and an 11º.

13 On one needle, pick up an 11º, and cross the other needle through it. On one needle, pick up 11 11ºs, and make a diamond shape as in step 10. End the threads.

14 Open a jump ring, and attach the clasp to the end loops.

For an adorable ring, make one component with a teardrop pendant crystal. Stitch a base of twin beads and seed beads: On 1 yd. (.9m) of thread, exit an 11º in the initial ring, and pick up a pattern of an 11º and a twin bead to the desired length. Sew through the component to exit the opposite side of the initial ring, and then pick up an 11º between the remaining holes of the twin beads. End the threads.

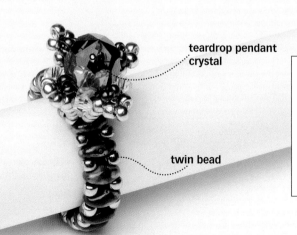

teardrop pendant crystal

twin bead

COLORS
- 6x11mm teardrop pendant crystal (Swarovski, tanzanite)
- 3mm bicone crystals (Swarovski, light azore)
- 11º seed beads (metallic sage)
- Twin beads (blue)

Tic-Tac Twins Bracelet

Twin beads create the delightful pattern of Xs in this bracelet. One strand is delicate; play with the idea and stitch several together for true elegance multiplied!

MATERIALS

Bracelet 7¼ in. (18.4cm)

- **30** 3mm bicone crystals (crystal satin)
- **64** twin beads (dark olive)
- **2–3 grams** 11º seed beads (matte green/brown)
- **1–2 grams** 15º seed beads (silver)
- **2** 6mm jump rings
- Clasp
- Fireline 6 lb. test
- Beading needles, #12

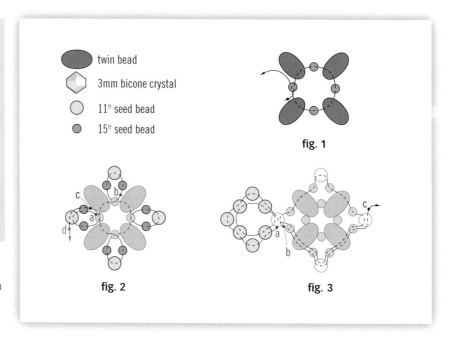

twin bead

3mm bicone crystal

11º seed bead

15º seed bead

fig. 1

fig. 2

fig. 3

1 On 2–3 yd. (1.8–2.7m) of Fireline, pick up a pattern of a 15º seed bead and one hole of a twin bead four times, leaving a 12-in. (30cm) tail. Sew through the first 15º to form a ring **[fig. 1]**. Retrace the thread path of the ring.

2 Exiting a 15º in the ring, pick up a 15º, an 11º, and a 15º, and sew through the 15º your thread exited at the start of this step again, the same hole of the first twin bead in the ring, and the next 15º **[fig. 2, a–b]**. Repeat this step three times, adding four picots **[b–c]**, and then exit the first two beads picked up in this step **[c–d]**.

3 Pick up seven 11ºs, and sew through the 11º your thread exited at the start of this step. Retrace the thread path of the new ring, skipping every other 11º to form a diamond shape **[fig. 3, a–b]**.

4 Sew through the beads added in step 2 and the remaining holes of the twin beads to anchor the picots to the twin beads. Exit the center 11º across from the new ring of 11ºs **[b–c]**. End the tail.

5 With the working thread, pick up three 15ºs, and sew through the 11º your thread exited at the start of this step and the first two 15ºs picked up in this step **[fig. 4]**.

6 Pick up a twin bead and a 15º three times, and then pick up a twin bead. Sew through the 15º your thread exited at the start of this step and the next twin bead and 15º in the new ring. Work as in step 2 to add three picots, exiting the first two beads picked up in step 5, and then work as in step 4 to anchor the new picots. Exit the center 11º across from the last join **[fig. 5]**.

7 Repeat steps 5 and 6 until you reach the desired length, and then work as in step 3 to add a second loop for the clasp. End the working thread.

8 Add 1 yd. (.9m) of thread to one end of the bracelet, and exit the outer hole of a twin bead in the first unit that is closest to the next unit. Pick up a 3mm bicone crystal, and sew through the outer hole of the closest twin bead in the next unit. Continue along this edge **[fig. 6]**. Repeat along the other edge.

9 Open a jump ring, and attach the clasp to the end loops.

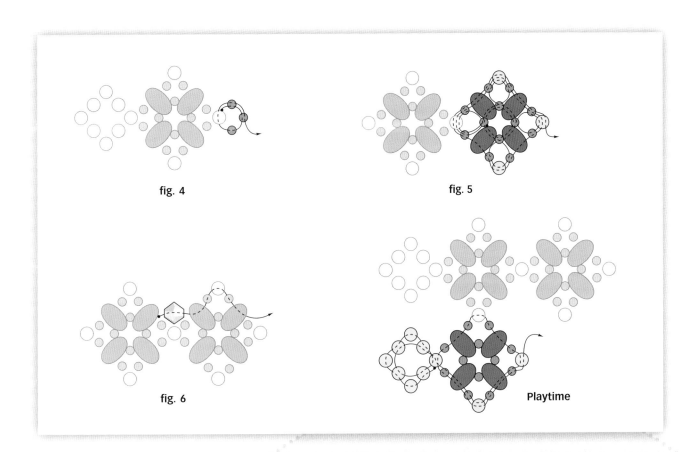

fig. 4

fig. 5

fig. 6

Playtime

COLORS

Triple-strand bracelet

- **168** twin beads (jet Picasso)
- **134** 3mm bicone crystals (purple velvet)
- 5 grams 11º seed beads (metallic purple)
- 4 grams 15º seed beads (metallic green)

Double-strand bracelet

- **120** twin beads (jet Picasso)
- **56** 3mm bicone crystals (light azore)
- 2–3 grams 11º seed beads (silver)
- 1–2 grams 15º seed beads (nickel plated)

To make multiple strands, work as in the first strand, but in step 2, sew through the center 11º from a side picot of the first strand instead of picking up a new 11º to connect the two strands [**figure**]. Add crystals in the same manner as in step 8 to all the strands, or fill in the spaces between every twin bead with a crystal, as in the wide version shown below.

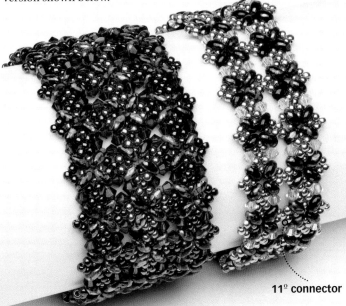

11º connector

Playtime

Playful Favorites

Delicate Net Bracelet

This delicate netted bracelet works well as everyday wear. Crystals are showcased toward the center of the bracelet; toward the ends, only pearls are captured in the netting.

MATERIALS
Gold iris bracelet 7¼ in. (18.4cm)
- **59** 3mm pearls (Swarovski, cyclamen opal)
- **18** 3mm round or bicone crystals (Swarovski, bronze)
- 3–5 grams 15º seed beads or cylinder beads (gold iris)
- Fireline 6 lb. test
- Beading needles, #12
- Clasp
- **2** jump rings

Purple bracelet
- 3mm pearls (Swarovski, mauve)
- 3mm bicone crystals (Swarovski, amethyst)
- 15º seed beads (transparent amethyst AB)

1 Attach a stop bead 10 in. (25cm) from the end of 2 yd. (1.8m) of Fireline. Pick up a 15º seed bead or cylinder bead, a 3mm pearl, six 15ºs, a pearl, and 11 15ºs. Sew back through the 15º above the last pearl picked up [**fig. 1**].

2 Pick up a pearl and five 15ºs. Sew through the 15º above the first pearl [**fig. 2**].

3 Pick up six 15ºs and a pearl, and sew back through the 15º above the last pearl [**fig. 3**].

4 Pick up five 15ºs and a pearl, and sew through the fifth 15º in the last row [**fig. 4**].

5 Pick up 10 15ºs, and sew back through the 15º above the last pearl [**fig. 5**].

6 Pick up a pearl and five 15ºs, and sew through the 15º above the pearl added in step 3 [**fig. 6**].

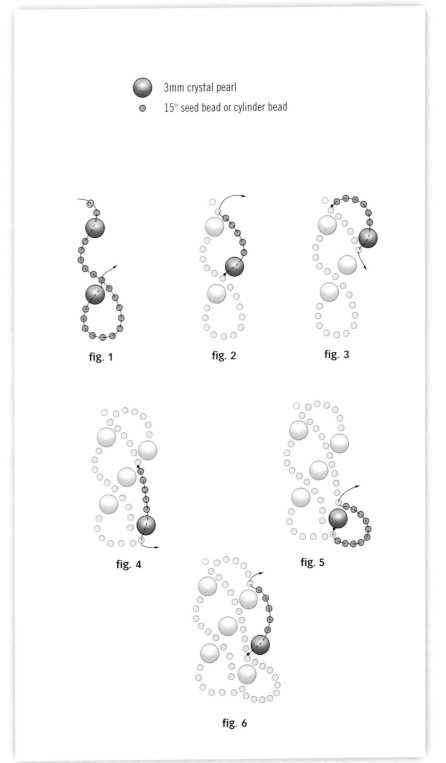

● 3mm crystal pearl

○ 15º seed bead or cylinder bead

fig. 1

fig. 2

fig. 3

fig. 4

fig. 5

fig. 6

7 Repeat steps 3–6 until you reach the desired length, starting with a 3mm crystal in the bottom stitch in step 4 and working steps 5, 6, and then 3 with crystals. Switch to pearls every other row for 11 rows or the centerpoint of the desired length. (You can always remove rows from the beginning if the center portion becomes too long.) Remove the stop bead, and end both tails, weaving the thread through the last few rounds and tying half-hitch knots. Attach half of a clasp to each end using jump rings.

COLORS
Blue bracelet
- 6mm round crystals (Swarovski, Indian sapphire)
- 11º charlottes (purple iris)

Crystal bracelet
- 6mm helix crystals (Swarovski, crystal)
- 11º seed beads (metallic gold iris)

To go from lightweight to bold, skip the pearls, bump up the crystals to 6mm, and use larger seed beads as in these two variations.

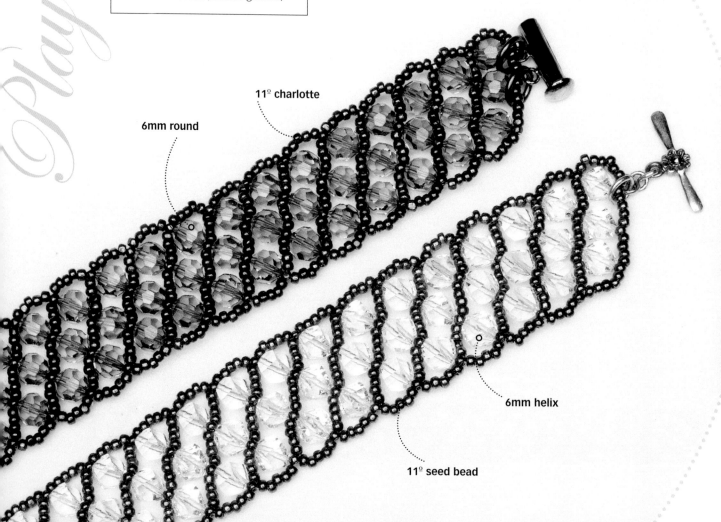

Playtime

11º charlotte

6mm round

11º seed bead

6mm helix

Lucky Charm Bracelet

This bracelet has a four-leaf clover motif down its center and lots of sparkling edging.

MATERIALS

Yellow bracelet
- About **150** 4mm bicone crystals (Swarovski, sand opal)
- 5–6 grams 8º seed beads (hybrid sour apple Picasso)
- 3–4 grams 11º seed beads (white opal)
- Gram 15º seed beads (silver-lined straw gold AB)
- Clasp
- Fireline 6 lb. test
- Beading needle, #12

Purple bracelet
- 4mm bicone crystals (Swarovski, cyclamen opal)
- 8º seed beads (matte teal iris)
- 11º seed beads (yellow-lined aqua AB)
- 15º seed beads (dark olivine)

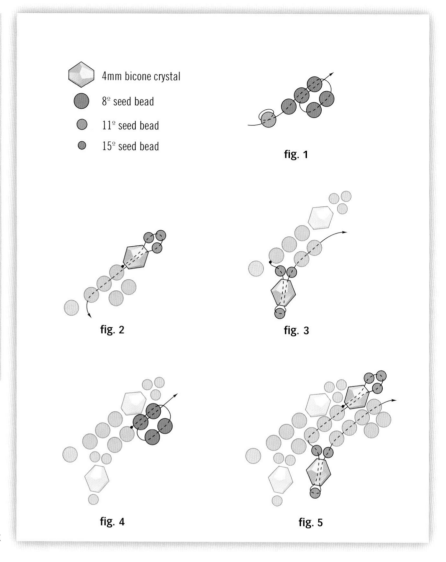

4mm bicone crystal

8º seed bead

11º seed bead

15º seed bead

fig. 1

fig. 2

fig. 3

fig. 4

fig. 5

1 On 2 yd. (1.8m) of Fireline, attach a stop bead, leaving a 6-in. (15cm) tail. Pick up five 8º seed beads, skip the first 8º picked up, and sew through the next two 8ºs. The last four 8ºs will sit next to each other in parallel stacks **[fig. 1]**.

2 Pick up a 4mm bicone crystal and three 11º seed beads. Skip the 11ºs, and sew back through the 4mm and the next three 8ºs in the stack your thread exited at the start of this step **[fig. 2]**.

3 Pick up an 11º, a 4mm, and an 11º*. Skip the last 11º, and sew back through the 4mm. Pick up an 11º, and sew through the two 8ºs in the next stack **[fig. 3]**.

*Note: When you work the second half of the bracelet, this 11º is the connecting point.

4 Pick up four 8ºs, and sew through the first two 8ºs just picked up, snugging the beads tight to the stack your thread exited at the start of this step. The last four 8ºs will sit next to each other in parallel stacks **[fig. 4]**.

5 Repeat steps 2–4 **[fig. 5]** until you reach the desired length. On the last repeat of step 4, pick up only two 8ºs instead of four, and then pick up a 4mm, and three 11ºs.

Skip the 11ºs, and sew back through the 4mm and the next four 8ºs in the end stack. End the working thread, remove the stop bead, and end the tail.

6 On a new 2-yd. (1.8m) length of Fireline, repeat steps 1–5, but in each repeat of step 3, sew through the corresponding 11º from the first stack instead of picking up a new one **[fig. 6]**.

7 On a new 1-yd. (.9m) length of Fireline, attach a stop bead, leaving a 10-in. (25cm) tail. Sew through the first center 11º on one end of the bracelet. Pick up a 15º and a 4mm, and sew through the next center 11º. Repeat down the length of the bracelet, exiting the last 11º.

8 Pick up 11 15ºs, half of the clasp, and 11 15ºs. Sew back through the center 11º

your thread exited at the start of this step, centering the clasp in the loop of 11 15ºs **[fig. 7]**.

9 Retrace the thread path through the center row, taking care not to pull too tight, or your bracelet might pucker.

10 Remove the stop bead, and attach the other half of the clasp on this end. Sew back through the center row, and reinforce the clasp on the other end. End the working thread.

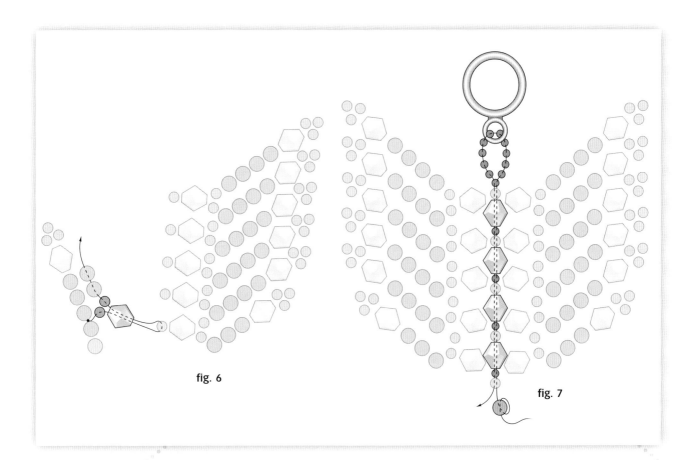

fig. 6

fig. 7

COLORS
- 3mm bicone crystals (Swarovski, crystal satin)
- 10º cylinder beads (matte pink/green)
- 15º seed beads (metallic bronze)
- Novelty button

Showcase a special button by making a button-and-loop clasp on a narrow version of this bracelet. Use 10º cylinder beads in place of 8º seed beads to make a narrower, more delicate band. Use 3mm crystals instead of 4mms and 15º seed beads instead of 11ºs, and attach a button to the pointed end. To make a loop on the other end, exit a stack of four 10º cylinder beads on one side of the end, pick up enough 15ºs to accommodate the button, and sew through the stack of four cylinders on the other side.

flower button

3mm bicone

10º cylinder bead

15º seed bead

The classic look of channel-set gemstones is perfect for any occasion. Make a stack and wear them together—easy tubular herringbone stitch works up in a jiff.

Channel-Set Crystals Bracelet

MATERIALS

Pink bracelet 7¼ in. (18.4cm)
- **90–100** 2mm round crystals (Swarovski, vintage rose)
- 4–6 grams 10º cylinder beads (matte pink/green)
- 2 grams 11º cylinder beads (matte pink/green)
- **2** 6mm jump rings
- Clasp
- Extender and dangles for clasp (optional)
- Fireline 6 lb. test
- Beading needles, #12 or #13

Green bracelet
- 2mm round crystals (Swarovski, crystal silver shade)
- 10º cylinder beads (dark green metallic iris)
- 11º cylinder beads (lined emerald AB)

Red bracelet
- 2mm round crystals (Swarovski, siam)
- 10º cylinder beads (blue/topaz AB)
- 11º cylinder beads (blue/topaz AB)

1 On 2½ yd. (2.3m) of Fireline, attach a stop bead, leaving a 12-in. (30cm) tail. Pick up an 11º cylinder bead and a 10º cylinder bead, and sew back through the 11º again so the two beads sit next to each other with the holes parallel. Sew through the 10º again **[fig. 1]**.

2 Pick up a 2mm round crystal, and sew through the previous 10º and the 2mm so the holes are parallel **[fig. 2]**.

3 Pick up a 10º, and sew through the 2mm and the new 10º so the holes are parallel **[fig. 3]**. Sew through the first 11º and the last 10º again to form a ring **[fig. 4]**.

4 Pick up a 10º and a 2mm, sew down through the 2mm in the previous round, and sew up through the next 10º **[fig. 5]**.

5 Pick up a 10º and an 11º, sew down through the next 11º in the previous round, and sew up through the next 10º. Step up through the 10º added in step 4 to be in position to begin the new round **[fig. 6]**.

6 Repeat steps 4 and 5 until you reach the desired length, maintaining tight, even tension. Work a thread path through the last round to snug it up.

7 Exiting a 10º, pick up five 10ºs, and sew down through the opposite 10º in the last round to make a loop. Retrace the thread path to reinforce the loop. End the working thread. Remove the stop bead, and repeat this step on the other end of the bracelet.

8 Attach one half of the clasp to the 10º loops on each end with jump rings.

TIP Make this bracelet adjustable by attaching several large (9mm), linked jump rings or a short piece of chain as an extender. Accent the extender with crystal dangles made with wrapped loops. See p. 79 for more information.

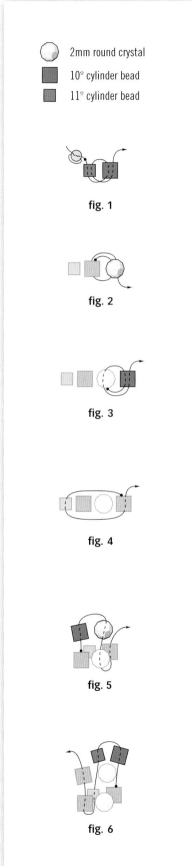

○ 2mm round crystal

■ 10º cylinder bead

■ 11º cylinder bead

fig. 1

fig. 2

fig. 3

fig. 4

fig. 5

fig. 6

COLORS

- 2mm round crystals (Swarovski, crystal moonlight)
- 10º cylinder beads (matte nickel)
- 11º cylinder beads (metallic green)

Double rows of channel-set crystals look stunning in this bangle version. Start with a ladder of a 10º, a 2mm, a 10º, a 2mm, a 10º, and three 11ºs. Exit the first 10º in the ladder, pick up a 10º and a 2mm for the first and second stitches, and then work two 11ºs per stitch for the next two stitches. Work until the beadwork fits around the largest part of your hand, and then zip up the first and last rounds to create a bangle.

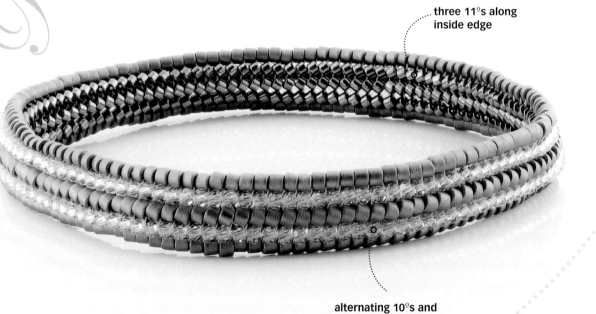

three 11ºs along inside edge

alternating 10ºs and 2mms along outside edge

Loopy Clasp Bracelet

In this bracelet, the toggle-and-ring clasp has a starring role alongside the right-angle weave base embellished with seed bead loops.

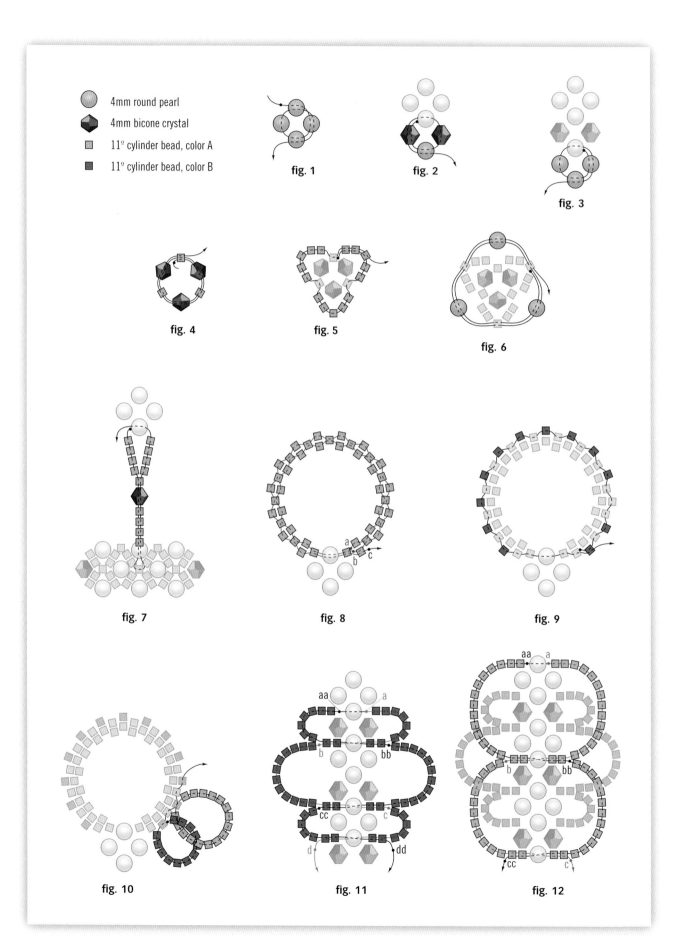

4mm round pearl

4mm bicone crystal

11º cylinder bead, color A

11º cylinder bead, color B

fig. 1

fig. 2

fig. 3

fig. 4

fig. 5

fig. 6

fig. 7

fig. 8

fig. 9

fig. 10

fig. 11

fig. 12

Make the base

1 On 2 yd. (1.8m) of Fireline, pick up four 4mm pearls, leaving a 12-in. (30cm) tail. Sew through the first three pearls again to make a ring [**fig. 1**].

2 Pick up a 4mm bicone crystal, a pearl, and a crystal. Sew back through the pearl your thread exited in the last step. Sew through the next crystal and pearl [**fig. 2**].

3 Pick up three pearls, and sew back through the pearl your thread exited in the last step. Sew through the next two pearls [**fig. 3**].

4 Repeat steps 2 and 3 until you reach the desired length minus about an inch for the clasp. Don't trim the working thread or tail. Set the base aside for now.

Make the toggle bar

5 On 1 yd. (.9m) of thread, make the toggle bar for the clasp: Pick up a pattern of one color-A cylinder bead and one 4mm bicone crystal three times, leaving a 6-in. (15cm) tail. Sew through all the beads again to form a ring, exiting an 11º [**fig. 4**].

6 Pick up five As, and sew through the next A in the ring. Repeat two more times. Step up through the first three As picked up in this step [**fig. 5**].

7 Pick up a pearl, skip five As, and sew through the next A. Repeat two more times [**fig. 6**], and then reinforce the pearl round by sewing through all the As and pearls in the round.

8 Repeat steps 6 and 7 five more times, but on the last round, use crystals instead of pearls. End the threads.

9 Using the shorter tail from the base of the bracelet, make sure the thread is exiting the end pearl. Pick up five As, a crystal, and four As, and sew through a center A in the toggle. Sew back through the four As, the crystal, and the next A. Pick up four As, and sew back through the last pearl in the base [**fig. 7**]. Retrace this thread path several times, and end the thread.

Attach the toggle loop

10 Using the tail on the other end of the base, make sure the thread is exiting the end pearl. Pick up 29 As to accommodate the toggle bar. Sew back through the end pearl again and the first A in the ring [**fig. 8, a–b**]. Work a round of peyote by picking up an A, skipping an A in the ring, and sewing through the next A. Repeat around the ring and step up through the first A in the new round [**b–c**].

11 Work another round of peyote using Bs. Sew through the first B added in this step [**fig. 9**].

12 Pick up 12 Bs, and sew through the B your thread exited at the beginning of this step and the next A and B in the peyote ring. Pick up 16 As and sew through the loop of Bs just completed, the B your thread is exiting, and the next A and B in the peyote ring [**fig. 10**]. Repeat around the ring, adding alternating loops of As and Bs. End the thread.

Add embellishment

13 Center 1 yd. (.9m) of Fireline in the second center pearl on the base of the bracelet. Thread a needle on each end, and pick up nine Bs on each needle. With each needle, cross through the next center pearl on the base, and sew through the last two Bs picked up on the other needle [**fig. 11, a–b and aa–bb**].

14 With each needle, pick up 14 Bs, skip a center pearl, cross through the next center pearl on the base, and sew through the last two Bs picked up on the other needle [**b–c and bb–cc**].

15 With each needle, pick up 7 Bs, cross through the next center pearl, and sew through the last two Bs picked up on the other needle [**c–d and cc–dd**].

16 Repeat steps 14 and 15 for the length of the bracelet, and end the threads.

MATERIALS
Teal bracelet 7½ in. (19.1cm)
- **79** 4mm round pearls (Swarovski, Tahitian look)
- **37** 4mm bicone crystals (Swarovski, light azore)
- 5 grams 11º cylinder beads or seed beads in each of two colors: Color A (nickel-plated) Color B (metallic silver)
- Fireline 6 lb. test
- Beading needles, #12 or #13

Dark green bracelet
- 4mm round pearls (Swarovski, Tahitian look)
- 4mm bicone crystals (Swarovski, light azore)
- Cylinder beads in two colors: Color A (dark green iris 15ºs) Color B (silver-plated 11ºs)

17 Start a new thread as in step 13, but center the Fireline in the end pearl. Pick up 17 As on each needle. Skip two center pearls, and cross through the next center pearl and the last two As picked up on the other needle [**fig. 12, a–b and aa–bb**].

18 With each needle, sew under the next set of loops made in the previous row of embellishment, pick up 15 As, skip two center pearls, and cross through the next center pearl and the last two As picked up on the other needle [**b–c and bb–cc**].

19 Repeat step 18 for the length of the bracelet, making sure the new loops pass through those made in the previous row of embellishment, and end the threads.

10mm pearl

SuperDuo

COLORS
- 10mm pearl (Swarovski, powder green)
- Cylinder beads:
  Color A (matte metallic dark green)
  Color B (transparent green rainbow)
- SuperDuo beads (green Picasso)

Make a ring out of the loopy clasp: Showcase a large pearl in the center and stitch a band with SuperDuo beads and seed beads. Begin with a ring of 32 color-A cylinder beads, and work one round of peyote stitch. Make loops as for the clasp of the Loopy Clasp Bracelet, p. 69, and then make a band as in the ring shown on p. 54.

Queen Anne's Necklace

Adorn yourself with lacy crystals cascading from a base of faceted pearls. Stringing and netting combine gracefully in this special-occasion necklace.

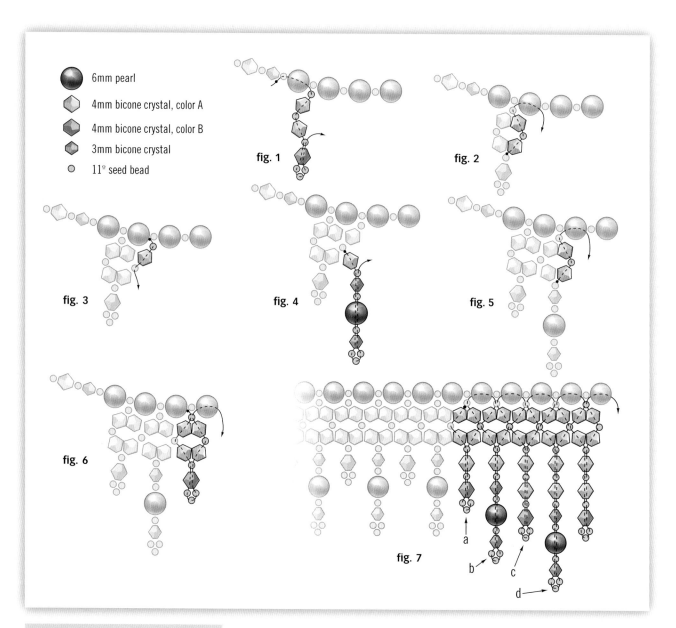

6mm pearl

4mm bicone crystal, color A

4mm bicone crystal, color B

3mm bicone crystal

11° seed bead

fig. 1

fig. 2

fig. 3

fig. 4

fig. 5

fig. 6

fig. 7

a

b

c

d

MATERIALS

Necklace 19 in. (48cm)

- **51** 6mm pearls (faceted blue)
- 4mm bicone crystals:
  132 color A (Swarovski, Indian sapphire)
  26 color B (Swarovski, violet)
- **38** 3mm bicone crystals (Swarovski, Montana)
- 5 grams 11° seed beads (transparent gray AB)
- Beading wire, .012–.014
- Fireline 6 lb. test
- Beading needles, #12
- 2 crimp beads
- Clasp

1 Temporarily secure one end of 20 in. (51cm) of flexible beading wire. String the necklace as follows: an 11° seed bead, a 3mm bicone crystal, an 11°, a color-B 4mm bicone crystal, an 11°, a 6mm pearl, an 11°, a color-A 4mm bicone crystal, an 11°, a B, an 11°, an A, an 11°, a 6mm, an 11°, a 3mm, an 11°, a B, an 11°, a B, an 11°, a 6mm, an 11°, a B, an 11°, an A, an 11°, a 3mm, an 11°, a 6mm, an 11°, a 3mm, an 11°, an A, an 11°, a B, an 11°, a 6mm, an 11°, a B, an 11°, an A, an 11°, a 3mm, and an 11°.

2 String a pattern of an 11° and a pearl until you have 28 pearls, ending with an 11°. String the other half of the necklace in a mirror image of the first. Temporarily secure the other end.

3 Thread a needle on 2 yd. (1.8m) of thread, and sew through the first 11° and 6mm of the pearl section, leaving a 10-in. (25cm) tail.

4 Pick up an 11°, an A, an 11°, an A, an 11°, a B, and three 11°s. Skip the last three 11°s, and sew back through the B and the next 11° **[fig. 1]**.

5 Pick up an A, an 11°, and an A. Sew through the first 11° picked up in the previous step and the next 6mm in the pearl section **[fig. 2]**. You will skip all the 11°s between the 6mms in the pearl section.

6 Pick up an 11° and an A, and sew through the side 11° picked up in the previous stitch **[fig. 3]**.

7 Pick up an A, an 11º, a 3mm, an 11º, a 6mm, an 11º, a 3mm, and three 11ºs. Skip the last three 11ºs, and sew back through the next six beads, exiting the first 11º picked up in this step **[fig. 4]**.

8 Pick up an A, an 11º, and an A. Sew through the first 11º picked up in the previous step and the next 6mm in the pearl section **[fig. 5]**.

9 Repeat step 6, and then pick up an A, an 11º, a B, and three 11ºs. Skip the last three 11ºs, and sew back through the B and the 11º above it. Repeat step 5 **[fig. 6]**.

10 Alternate steps 6–8 with step 9 until you have five short and five long dangles.

11 Make four dangles that graduate in size to the longest center dangle: For the next short dangle, repeat step 6, and pick up an A, an 11º, an A, an 11º, a B, and three 11ºs. Skip the three 11ºs, and sew back through the B, the 11º, the A, and the next 11º. Repeat steps 5 and 6 **[fig. 7, a]**. Add an extra A and 11º to the next long dangle in the

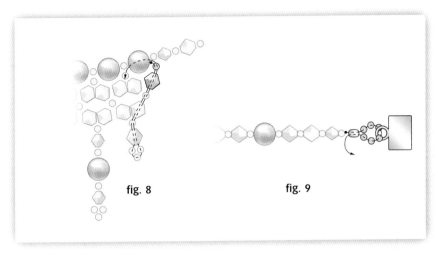

fig. 8

fig. 9

same manner as before **[b]**. For the next two fringe, add two extra As and 11ºs **[c and d]**. The last fringe completed is the centerpoint of the necklace.

12 Work the second half of the necklace as a mirror image of the first, exiting the last pearl in the pearl section.

13 To finish the ends of the woven section, pick up an 11º and an A, and sew through the side 11º from the last stitch **[fig. 8]**.

Retrace the thread path of the last dangle, and end the thread. Repeat on the other end with the tail.

14 To finish the ends of the necklace, string a crimp bead, three 11ºs, half of the clasp, and three 11ºs. Go back through the crimp bead **[fig. 9]**, and snug up the beads. Crimp the crimp bead, and trim the excess wire. Repeat on the other end.

COLORS
- 5mm pearls (Swarovski, dark green)
- 4mm bicone crystals (Swarovski, black diamond)
- 4mm bicone crystals (Swarovski, garnet)
- 11º seed beads (transparent gray luster)

Make a cute coordinating pair of earrings: Pick up an 11º, a 3mm, an 11º, a 4mm, an 11º, a 4mm, an 11º, a 5mm pearl, an 11º, a 4mm, and three 11ºs. Skip the last three 11ºs, and sew back through the next 4mm, 11º, 5mm, and 11º. Pick up a 4mm, an 11º, and a 4mm, skip a 4mm, 11º, and 4mm, and sew through the next 11º, 3mm, and 11º. Pick up a soldered jump ring, and sew back through the last 11º, 3mm, and 11º. Pick up a 4mm, 11º, and 4mm, skip a 4mm, 11º, and 4mm, and sew through the next 11º, 5mm, 11º, 4mm, and three 11ºs. Retrace the thread path and end the thread. Make a second earring.

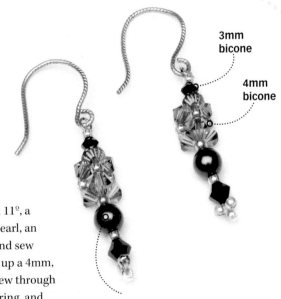

3mm bicone

4mm bicone

5mm pearl

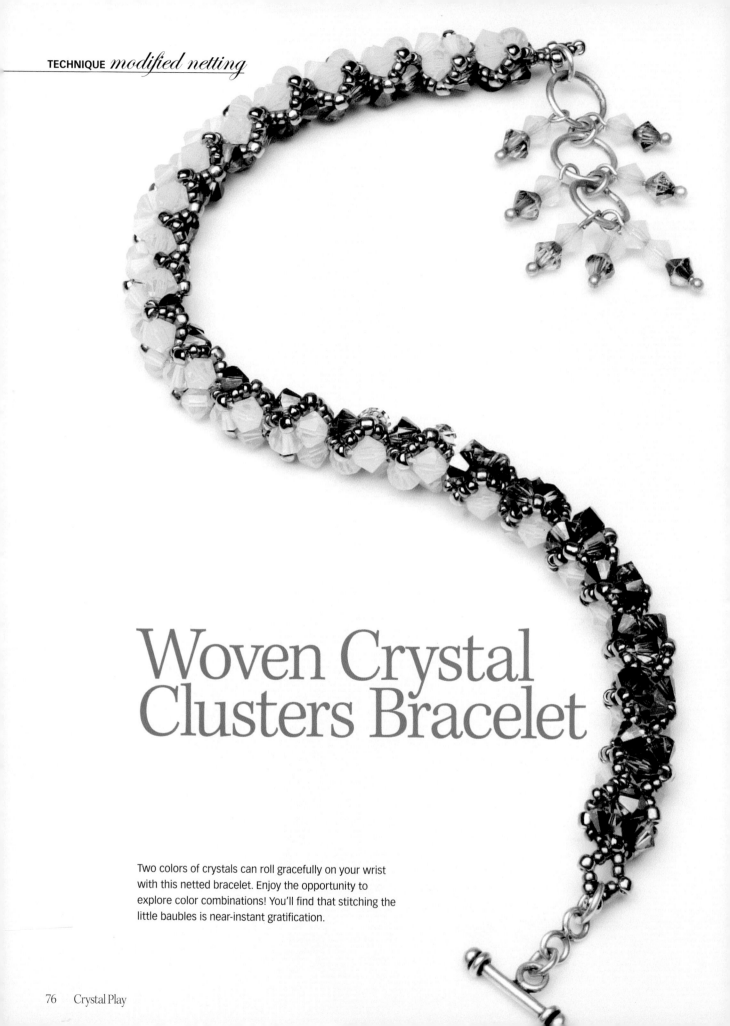

Woven Crystal
Clusters Bracelet

Two colors of crystals can roll gracefully on your wrist
with this netted bracelet. Enjoy the opportunity to
explore color combinations! You'll find that stitching the
little baubles is near-instant gratification.

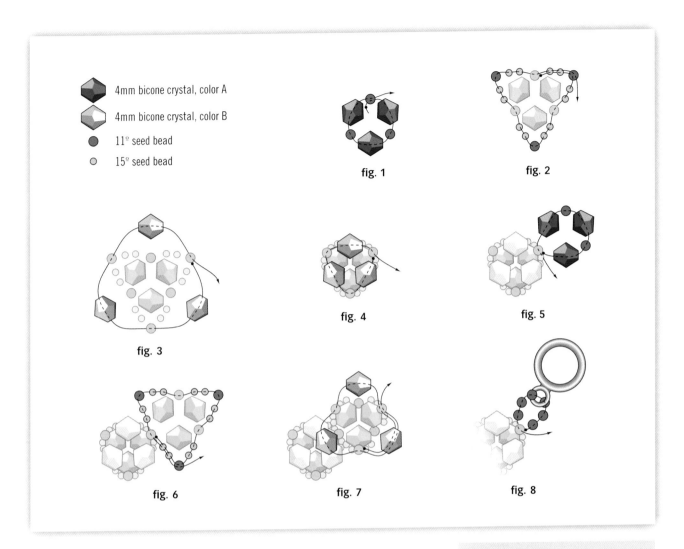

Legend:
- 4mm bicone crystal, color A
- 4mm bicone crystal, color B
- 11º seed bead
- 15º seed bead

fig. 1

fig. 2

fig. 3

fig. 4

fig. 5

fig. 6

fig. 7

fig. 8

1 On 3 yd. (2.7m) of Fireline, pick up a pattern of an 11º seed bead and a color-A 4mm bicone crystal three times, leaving a 12-in. (30cm) tail. Sew back through the first 11º **[fig. 1]**, and retrace the thread path to reinforce the crystal round.

2 Pick up two 15º seed beads, an 11º, and two 15ºs, and sew through the next 11º in the previous round. Repeat two more times, and step up through the first two 15ºs and 11º added in this round **[fig. 2]**.

3 Pick up a color-B 4mm bicone crystal, and sew through the next 11º in the previous round. Repeat twice, and reinforce the round, exiting an 11º **[figs. 3 and 4]**.

4 The next cluster will be attached to the first. Pick up an A, an 11º, an A, an 11º, and an A. Sew back through the 11º your thread exited at the start of this step **[fig. 5]**. Reinforce the round.

5 Pick up two 15ºs, an 11º, and two 15ºs. Sew through the next 11º in the previous round. Repeat two more times, and step up through the first two 15ºs and 11º added in this step **[fig. 6]**.

6 Pick up a B, and sew through the next 11º in the previous round. Repeat twice and reinforce. Sew through the 11º opposite the previous cluster **[fig. 7]**.

7 Repeat steps 4–6 until the bracelet is the desired length, minus the length of the clasp.

8 Pick up three 11ºs, half of the clasp, and three 11ºs **[fig. 8]**. Retrace the thread path, and end the threads. Repeat this step with the tail and the other half of the clasp.

MATERIALS

Bracelet 7¾ in. (19.7cm)
- 4mm bicone crystals:
  72 color A (Swarovski, white opal)
  72 color B (Swarovski, Bermuda blue)
- 2 grams 11º seed beads (silver)
- 4 grams 15º seed beads (silver)
- Fireline 6 lb. test
- Beading needles, #12
- Clasp
- Extender and dangles for clasp (optional)

TIP It's easy to make this bracelet adjustable if you use a toggle bar on one end and attach several large (9mm), linked jump rings or a piece of large-link chain to the other. Use extra crystals to make dangles. See p. 79 for other ideas.

COLORS
- 6mm lentil crystals (Swarovski, cyclamen opal)
- 4mm bicone crystals (Swarovski, blue zircon)
- 11º seed beads (blue)
- 15º seed beads (purple)

Using lentil-shaped crystals in place of color-B bicones entirely changes the look of this versatile design.

6mm lentil

Ask Anna

Anna's fans often go to her for help with pesky beading problems. Here she addresses a few questions and explains how she creates a few features that make her designs versatile and wearable.

Q **I give jewelry as gifts, and I don't always know the exact size to use. How can I make my jewelry adjustable?**

A I used extenders in several projects in this book: the Northern Lights Necklace (p. 39), the Channel-Set Crystals Bracelet (p. 66), and the Woven Crystal Clusters Bracelet (p. 76). An extender is adjustable, plus it's also an easy way to lengthen a project by an inch or so. For example, in Channel-Set Crystals, I show two types of extenders: one made of linked large rings that act as loops for a small toggle bar and one that uses a short length of chain that hooks into a spring clasp. For the rings, you can use large (9–10mm) soldered jump rings and link them with small open jump rings, or simply use a short length of large-link chain.

Adding dangles to the extender looks pretty—they integrate the extender into the jewelry design. To make a dangle, string a bead or crystal on a headpin, make the first part of a wrapped loop, attach the loop to your jump ring or chain, and finish the loop.

Q **My wrists must be a lot bigger than yours! I always need to enlarge a bracelet from the size given in the instructions. Can you give me some tips on how to do this?**

A It's good to pay attention to this before you start stitching! Lengthening bracelets (and necklaces too) is fairly easy if the project is a simple flat weave; just check the length as you stitch, and add what you need. If the bracelet features a pattern or a series of components, you will probably be able to repeat just one element or add a component to get the size you need. After you've stitched part of the design, look for a repeatable part of the pattern that you can add to get the length you need. Bumping up all the bead sizes is another way to make a design larger and a bit bolder.

Adjusting a bangle size from directions is similar. To get your target size, hold your hand as though you are sliding it through the bangle, and wrap a flexible tape measure around the widest part of your hand. A bangle has to fit over your hand at

this point, but you don't want it sliding off as you wear it, so measure carefully. Double check the size by measuring a bangle you own that fits nicely.

If you're using Fireline and your tension is tight, your jewelry piece won't grow after you've worn it awhile. If your tension is loose and you can see thread between beads, the bracelet or bangle will spread as you wear it; retrace thread paths to tighten up the work.

Q **I'm an impatient beader. I hate to take the time to constantly add thread and end tails in my work, but I hate tangled thread even more! Any suggestions?**

A Working with a comfortable length of about 1–2 yd. (1.4–1.8m) of thread will help keep your thread from tangling. If you try to use enough thread to complete every project, you will probably spend as much time undoing knots and pulling yards of thread through each stitch as you would ending and adding shorter lengths.

Q **Can I just make a few knots to end my thread?**

A It's important to weave through the last several rows of stitches and make a few half-hitch knots as you go to secure your thread in the beadwork rather than just tying several knots. If the knots come out but you've sewn back through the beadwork, the work won't come undone. This is important whenever you add thread, and it's especially necessary when adding clasps.

Q **In a lot of your designs, you attach a clasp to a beaded loop that extends from the beadwork. Can you explain why and how you do this?**

A I like the point of attachment to be covered with beads. That way it won't be a weak spot where the metal clasp rubs on bare thread. The Woven Crystal Clusters project uses this technique. You can form shapes like diamonds by skipping some of the beads in the loop: Pick up the desired number of beads for the size of loop needed, and then decide which beads need to be skipped to form the shape. For instance, if you have 12 beads in the loop, sew through the first three beads to form the loop. Skip the next bead, sew through the next two beads in the loop, skip the next, sew through the next two, skip the next, and sew through the next two. Pull tight to make the skipped beads pop out, forming the diamond shape. Making shaped loops works well when adding a clasp with jump rings, but make sure the loop is pulled tight and the beads sit close together so the jump rings don't slip through.

Another
Dimension

Beehive Bangle

Construct a sturdy bangle that showcases crystals, pearls, and bugle beads in intriguing layers.

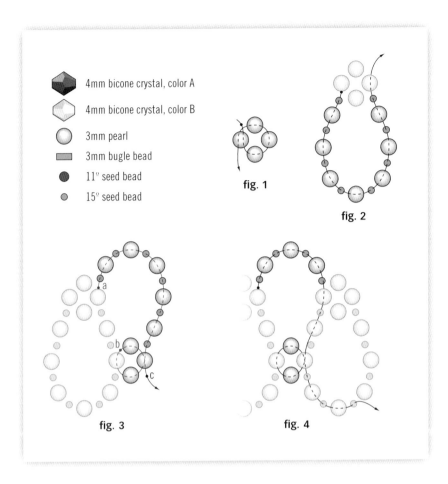

4mm bicone crystal, color A

4mm bicone crystal, color B

3mm pearl

3mm bugle bead

11º seed bead

15º seed bead

fig. 1

fig. 2

fig. 3

fig. 4

MATERIALS
Bangle 7¼ in. (18.4cm)
- 4mm bicone crystals:
  162 color A (Swarovski, mocha)
  46 color B (Swarovski, crystal golden shade)
- **208** 3mm pearls (Swarovski, gold)
- 15–20 grams 3mm bugle beads (beige)
- 5–6 grams 11º seed beads (brown)
- 3–5 grams 15º seed beads (brown)
- Fireline 6 lb. test
- Beading needles, #12

1 On 2 yd. (1.8m) of Fireline, pick up four 3mm pearls. Sew through the 3mms again to form a ring, leaving a 6-in. (15cm) tail [**fig. 1**].

2 Pick up a pattern of a 15º seed bead and a 3mm seven times, and then pick up a 15º. Sew through the opposite 3mm in the initial ring where your thread exited at the start of this step [**fig. 2**].

3 Pick up a pattern of a 15º and a 3mm six times, and then pick up a 3mm. Sew back through the sixth 3mm picked up in the previous step [**fig. 3, a–b**], pick up a 3mm, and sew through the sixth 3mm picked up in this step [**b–c**]. This creates a right-angle weave connecting unit.

4 Pick up a pattern of a 15º and a 3mm six times, and then pick up a 3mm. Sew back through the fourth 3mm picked up in the previous step, pick up a 3mm, and sew through the sixth 3mm picked up in this step.

5 Repeat step 4 until the strip of beadwork is long enough to fit around the largest part of your hand. Join the base together as shown [**fig. 4**]. End the threads.

6 Add a new thread to the base, exiting a 3mm. Pick up a 15º, a bugle bead, a 15º, a color-A 4mm bicone crystal, a 15º, a bugle, and a 15º. Sew back through the 3mm your thread exited at the start of this stitch and the next 15º and 3mm in the base **[fig. 5, a–b]**.

7 Pick up a 15º, a bugle, a 15º, and an A, and sew back through the nearest 15º, bugle, and 15º in the previous stitch. Sew back through the 3mm your thread exited at the start of this stitch and the next 15º and 3mm in the base **[b–c]**. Repeat this step, following the established chevron chain pattern in the base, leaving the two 3mms added in step 3 in the right-angle weave connecting unit without embellishment. Join the first and last stitch by picking up only an A and sewing through the existing 15ºs and bugles. End and add thread as needed.

8 Exiting a top A, pick up an 11º seed bead, and sew through the next A. Continue adding 11º between existing As. When you reach an A above a 3mm right-angle weave

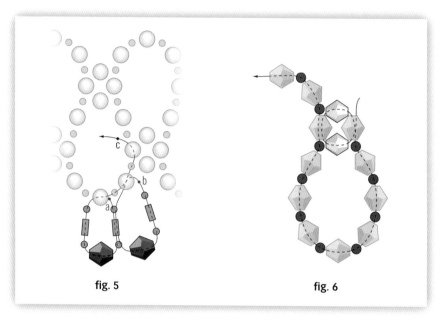

fig. 5

fig. 6

connecting unit, pick up a color-B 4mm bicone crystal, sew through the A opposite the connecting unit, pick up a B, and sew through the first A to create a connecting unit along the top surface **[fig. 6]**. Continue as in this step to embellish the top with 11ºs and add connecting units.

COLORS
- 4mm round pearls and crystals in place of 3mm base pearls:
  84 color A (Swarovski, light green)
  46 color B (Swarovski, cream)
- **79** 4mm bicone crystals (Swarovski, chrysolite satin)
- **132** 5mm bicone crystals in place of 4mm top-layer crystals
- **46** color-A pearls in place of 4mm color-B top-layer crystals
- 6mm twisted bugle beads (nickel)
- 11º seed beads (jet)
- 15º seed beads (off-white luster)

Create interest by using other shapes and colors in the layers. In this variation, I used 6mm twisted bugles, 4mm crystals along the edges of the base, and 5mm crystals on the outside.

Playtime

11º seed bead

6mm twisted bugle bead

5mm bicone

The slinky underbelly of this bangle reminds me of my sister's pet snake. But don't let that deter you if you're not fond of serpents—this bracelet won't bite! SuperDuo beads nestle so nicely together, and they provide the perfect base for a band of crystal embellishments.

Snake-Belly Bangle

MATERIALS

Blue bangle 7½ in. (19.1cm)
- **36–40** 4mm bicone crystals (Montana)
- **180–200** 3mm bicone crystals (Indian sapphire)
- **240–300** SuperDuo beads (multi blue)
- 2–3 grams 11º cylinder beads (nickel)
- Fireline 6 lb. test
- Beading needles, #12

Cream bangle
- 4mm bicone crystals (Swarovski, chrysolite satin)
- 3mm bicone crystals (Swarovski, sand opal)
- SuperDuo beads (cream)
- 11º cylinder beads (olive lined)

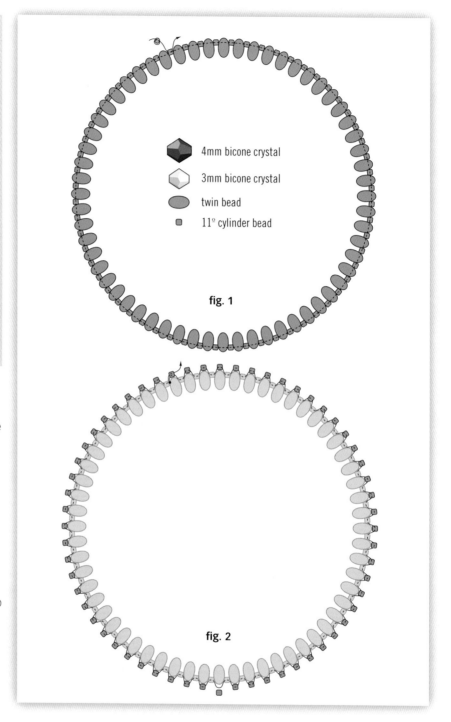

4mm bicone crystal

3mm bicone crystal

twin bead

11º cylinder bead

fig. 1

fig. 2

1 On 2 yd. (1.8m) of Fireline, attach a stop bead, leaving a 6-in. (15cm) tail. Pick up a pattern of an 11º cylinder bead and one hole of a SuperDuo bead 60 times, or enough times to fit around the largest part of your hand, ending with an even number. Sew through the first 11º again to make a ring **[fig. 1]**.

2 Work a round of circular peyote stitch by picking up an 11º, skipping a SuperDuo bead in the ring, and sewing through the next 11º in the ring. Repeat around the ring, using slightly loose but even tension. Step up through the first 11º picked up in this round **[fig. 2]**.

3 Work a round of circular peyote stitch using SuperDuo beads **[fig. 3]**, and end the threads.

4 Add a new thread to the remaining hole of a base SuperDuo bead from step 1. Pick up an 11º, and sew through the remaining hole of the next base SuperDuo bead. Repeat to complete the round.

5 Repeat steps 2 and 3 on this side of the base beads.

6 Add a new thread to a remaining hole of a SuperDuo bead along one of the outer edges. Pick up three 3mm bicone crystals, and sew through the same SuperDuo bead again. Sew through the first two 3mms just picked up. Pick up a 3mm, and sew through the remaining hole of the SuperDuo bead opposite the one your thread exited at the start of this step. Pick up a 3mm, and sew through the center 3mm from the first stitch. Sew through the first 3mm picked up in this

stitch and the remaining hole in the next SuperDuo bead along this edge **[fig. 4]**.

7 Continue in right-angle weave as in step 6, but in the first stitch, pick up a 3mm, a 4mm bicone crystal, and a 3mm **[fig. 5]**.

8 Alternate using all 3mms as in step 6 with step 7 until you fill the space between the remaining SuperDuo beads, ending and adding thread as needed.

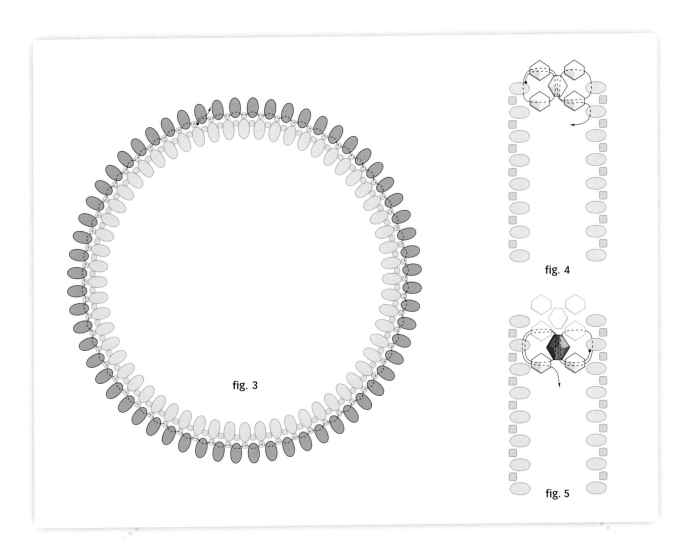

fig. 3

fig. 4

fig. 5

An extra round of right-angle weave and an exotic color palette result in a bold, beautiful bangle. Work three rows of 10º cylinder beads between steps 2 and 3. For the crystal embellishment that starts in step 6, work three stitches of right-angle weave between the edge SuperDuos.

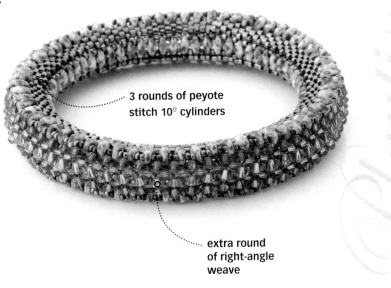

3 rounds of peyote stitch 10º cylinders

extra round of right-angle weave

COLORS

- 4mm bicone crystals (Swarovski, light olivine)
- 3mm bicone crystals (Swarovski, olivine)
- SuperDuo beads (multi brown)
- 11º cylinder beads (green AB)
- 10º cylinder beads (green iris)

Bejeweled Bangle

Catch a treasure trove of crystals and pearls within this modified tubular netted rope. The embellished peyote tube hides a magnetic clasp.

MATERIALS

Pink bangle 8 in. (20cm)

- **40–60** each:
  5mm or 6mm bicone crystals (Swarovski, fuchsia)
  5mm oval pearls (natural pearls, cream)
  4mm round pearls (Swarovski, light peach)
  4mm bicone crystals (Swarovski, light rose champagne)
- 20 grams 15º seed beads (lined cranberry)
- Flower button (optional)
- Magnetic clasp
- Fireline 4 or 6 lb. test
- Beading needles, #12

Dark red bangle

- 5mm or 6mm bicone crystals (Swarovski, light rose satin)
- 5mm oval pearls (natural pearls, dark cream)
- 4mm round pearls (dark pink)
- 4mm bicone crystals (Swarovski, light rose satin)
- 15º seed beads (cranberry)

1 On 3 yd. (2.7m) of Fireline, pick up a 15º seed bead, a 4mm bicone crystal, a 15º, a 4mm bicone crystal, a 15º, and a 4mm bicone crystal. Sew back through the first 15º picked up to make a tight ring **[fig. 1]**, and then reinforce the ring with a second thread path. Exit a 15º.

2 Pick up seven 15ºs, skip the next crystal in the ring, and sew through the following 15º. Repeat this stitch twice, and then step up through the first four 15ºs picked up in the first stitch **[fig. 2]**. You do not need to reinforce the 15º rounds, but you can if you have trouble keeping even tension. Just be sure to exit the center 15º before starting the next crystal or pearl round.

3 Pick up a 4mm pearl, and sew through the center 15º in the next set of seven 15ºs. Repeat this step twice **[fig. 3]**, and reinforce this round with a second thread path. Always reinforce the accent bead rounds.

4 Continue the next 10 rounds as in steps 2 and 3, changing the number of 15ºs and the accent beads as follows:
Seed bead round (seven 15ºs per stitch)
5mm oval pearl round
15º round (increase to nine 15ºs per stitch)
5 or 6mm crystal round
15º round (nine 15ºs)
5mm pearl round
15º round (seven 15ºs)
4mm pearl round
15º round (seven 15ºs)
4mm crystal round

5 Repeat the accent bead round sequence as in steps 3 and 4 until you reach the desired length. End with a 4mm crystal round.

6 Stitch a magnetic clasp to the ends of the tube, tightly securing the clasp in place. End the threads.

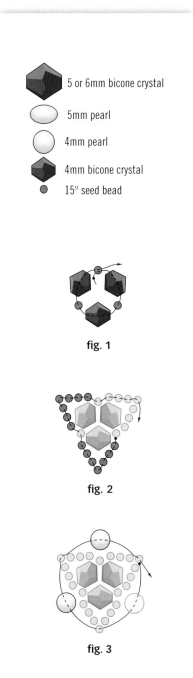

5 or 6mm bicone crystal

5mm pearl

4mm pearl

4mm bicone crystal

15º seed bead

fig. 1

fig. 2

fig. 3

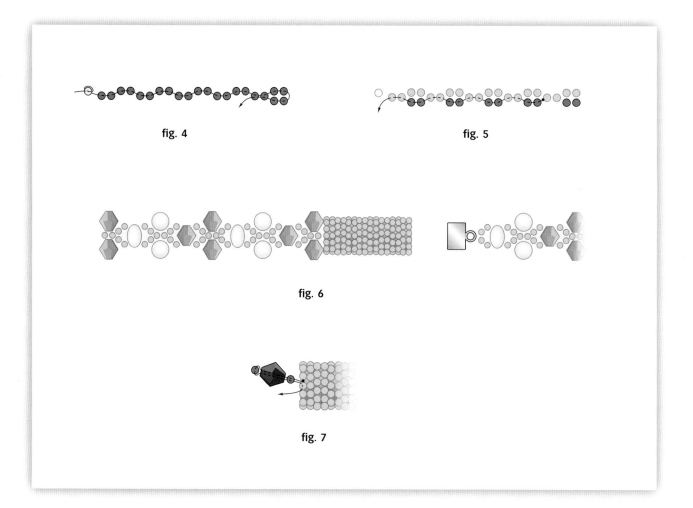

fig. 4

fig. 5

fig. 6

fig. 7

7 On 2 yd. (1.8m) of Fireline, attach a stop bead and make a two-drop peyote strip by picking up 22 15ºs. Skip the last four 15ºs and sew through the next two **[fig. 4]**.

8 For each subsequent stitch, pick up two 15ºs, skip two 15ºs, and sew through the next two 15ºs **[fig. 5]**. Keep adding rows until this strip is long enough to wrap around the end of the netted tube. Make sure the tails end up on the opposite ends of the strip.

9 Zip up the ends of the strip to form a tube.

10 Slide the tube over the magnetic clasp on one end of the bracelet. Make sure that when the bracelet is clasped, the magnets do not show. Stitch the tube to the bracelet two or three rounds from one end **[fig. 6]**.

11 Make short fringe on the ends of the tube: Exit a bead on the edge, and pick up a 15º, a crystal or pearl, and a 15º. Skip the last 15º, and sew back through the crystal or pearl, the 15º, and the edge 15º. Sew through the next 15º on the edge **[fig. 7]**. Repeat to make 5–6 additional fringe, picking up different crystals and pearls for each fringe. Repeat on the other edge of the tube.

12 Stitch the flower to a center bead in the tube, and make short fringe in the center of the flower as desired.

COLORS

- 6mm bicone crystals (Swarovski, light amethyst)
- 6mm keshi pearls (natural pearls/dyed green-blue)
- 10º triangle beads (transparent gray AB)

Use 10º triangle beads and alternate rounds of 6mm bicone crystals with keshi pearls for an organic, ocean-inspired version. Join the ends of the netted tube without a clasp.

6mm lentil

10º triangle

keshi pearl

Netted Elegance Bracelet

Choose crystals or pearls as you make loops to adorn a comfortable netted base.

1 On 3½ yd. (3.2m) of Fireline, attach a stop bead, leaving a 1½ yd. (1.4m) tail. Pick up 17 15º seed beads, a 2mm round crystal, and four 15ºs. Skip the last nine beads, and sew back through the next 15º. Pick up five 15ºs, skip five 15ºs, and sew though the next 15º. Pick up five 15ºs, skip five 15ºs, and sew through the first 15º **[fig. 1]**.

2 Pick up a 15º, a 2mm, and four 15ºs. Skip three 15ºs in the previous row (counting the bead your thread exited at the start of this step), and sew back through the next 15º. Pick up five 15ºs, skip five 15ºs, and sew through the next 15º. Pick up 15ºs, skip five

15ºs, and sew through the next 15º **[fig. 2]**. Repeat this step until you reach the desired length, minus the length of the clasp.

3 Using the tail, exit **[fig. 3, point a]** at the top of this connector bead, and then pick up loop 1. Lay the beads across the band, count 10 15ºs in the diagonal row, and then sew up through four 15ºs **[a–b]**. Sew through the next six 15ºs, along the next diagonal row **[b–c]**. Pick up loop 2, cross the band, and sew through the next 10 beads. Repeat across the surface, alternating between loop 1 and 2. End the threads.

Loop 1: Pick up a 15º, a 3mm bicone crystal, a 15º, a 4mm bicone crystal, a 15º, a 3mm, and a 15º.

Loop 2: Pick up two 15ºs, a 3mm, a 15º, a 4mm, a 15º, a 3mm, and two 15ºs.

4 Open a jump ring, and attach a loop of the clasp to an end loop of 15ºs. Repeat to attach all the loops of the clasp on both ends.

MATERIALS
Brown/gold bracelet 7 in. (18cm)
- **40–50** 4mm bicone crystals (Swarovski, garnet satin)
- **80–100** 3mm bicone crystals (Swarovski, metallic light gold)
- **80–100** 2mm round crystals (Swarovski, light Colorado topaz)
- 3–5 grams 15º seed beads (gold-lined AB)
- Multistrand clasp
- **4** 6mm jump rings
- Fireline 6 lb. test
- Beading needles, #12 or #13

Green bracelet
- 3mm pearls in place of 4mm bicones (Swarovski, powder green)
- 3mm bicone crystals (Swarovski, purple haze)
- 11º seed beads in place of 2mm round crystals (metallic green)
- 15º seed beads (green AB)

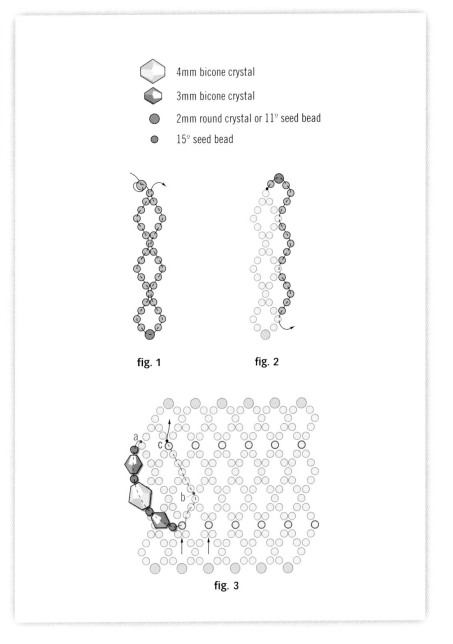

4mm bicone crystal

3mm bicone crystal

2mm round crystal or 11º seed bead

15º seed bead

fig. 1   fig. 2

fig. 3

3mm bicone

11º seed bead

Playtime

Step up the sizes for a bigger, bolder bracelet. Use 11º seed beads in place of the 15ºs and 3mm bicone crystals in place of the 2mms. Keep 3mms and 4mms in the loops.

COLORS
- 4mm bicone crystals (Swarovski, purple velvet)
- 3mm bicone crystals (Swarovski, purple velvet/violet)
- 11º seed beads (purple opal-lined)

Flat-out Fabulous Bracelet

In this simple yet stunning design, you'll layer crystals over a base made of glass pony beads.

MATERIALS

Bracelet 7½ in. (19.1cm)
- **35** 5mm glass pony beads (fuchsia lined)
- **420** 4mm crystal bicone crystals (Swarovski, fuchsia)
- 3–4 grams 11º seed beads (teal)
- **2** crimp beads
- **2** crimp covers
- Clasp
- Beading wire, .012–.014
- Fireline 6 lb. test
- Beading needles, #12
- Bead Stopper or tape

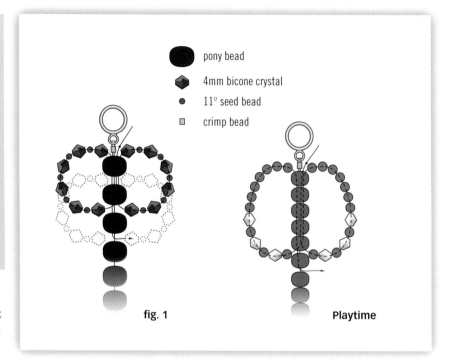

pony bead

4mm bicone crystal

11º seed bead

crimp bead

fig. 1

Playtime

1 On 12 in. (30cm) of beading wire, string a crimp bead and one half of a clasp. Go back through the crimp bead, leaving a short tail. Crimp the crimp bead. String 35 glass pony beads. Temporarily secure the end of the beading wire with a Bead Stopper or tape.

2 On 2 yd. (1.8m) of Fireline, attach a stop bead, leaving a 10-in. (25cm) tail. Sew through the first two pony beads, and pick up a pattern of a 4mm bicone crystal and an 11º seed bead five times. Then pick up a

4mm. Sew back through the first two pony beads again. Repeat to make a second loop, pushing each loop to one side. Sew through the next pony bead.

3 Continue making two loops for each pair of pony beads as in step 2, sewing

through three pony beads each time you add the second loop **[fig. 1]**. End and add thread as needed.

4 Remove the stopper and add the other half of the clasp to the beading wire as in step 1.

8º seed bead

Use 8º seed beads in place of crystals for a smooth interior to rest on your skin. For the first half of each loop, pick up seven 8ºs, and then pick up a pattern of a 4mm and an 8º three times **[figure]**.

COLORS
- 5mm glass pony beads (purple lined)
- 4mm bicone crystals (Swarovski, Indian sapphire)
- 8º seed beads (metallic dark silver)

Playtime

Right-Angle Rendezvous Bracelet

Create stacked bugle-bead bezels to frame 6mm crystals or pearls. The frames alternate with pearl-and-seed-bead cubes that sit *en pointe* on the wrist.

MATERIALS

Green bracelet 7¾ in. (19.7cm)

- **11** 6mm round crystals (Swarovski, Indian sapphire)
- **88** 6mm twisted bugle beads (matte green)
- **64** 3mm crystal pearls (Swarovski, Tahitian look)
- 4–5 grams 11º seed beads (aqua)
- 2–3 grams 15º seed beads (silver-lined)
- **2** jump rings
- Clasp
- Fireline 6 lb. test
- Beading needles, #12 or #13

Gold bracelet

- 6mm crystal pearls in place of round crystals (Swarovski, light green)
- 6mm twisted bugle beads (silver-lined light green)
- 3mm crystal pearls (Swarovski, bright gold)
- 11º seed beads (transparent light green)
- 15º seed beads (light green)

1 Thread a needle on each end of 3 yd. (2.7m) of Fireline, and center a 3mm pearl. With one needle, pick up an 11º seed bead and a 3mm pearl. With the other needle, pick up an 11º, and cross through the last pearl picked up on the other needle **[fig. 1]**.

2 With one needle, pick up an 11º and a 3mm. With the other needle, pick up an 11º, and cross through the last pearl picked up on the other needle **[fig. 2]**.

3 With one needle, pick up an 11º seed bead and a 3mm pearl. With the other needle, pick up an 11º, and cross through the last pearl picked up with the other needle **[fig. 3]**.

4 With each needle, pick up an 11º, and cross the needles through the first 3mm **[fig. 4]**. With each needle, sew through the 11ºs and pearls to exit the 3mm opposite the tail.

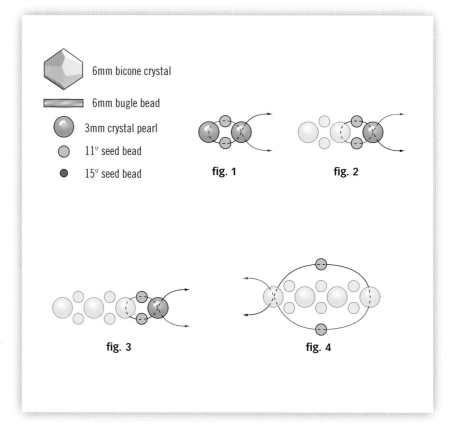

6mm bicone crystal

6mm bugle bead

3mm crystal pearl

11º seed bead

15º seed bead

fig. 1

fig. 2

fig. 3

fig. 4

5 With one needle, pick up a 6mm bugle bead and a 3mm. With the other needle, pick up a bugle bead, and cross through the last 3mm picked up with the other needle **[fig. 5]**. Repeat this step two more times **[fig. 6]**.

6 With each needle, pick up a bugle bead, and cross both needles through the end 3mm in the previous cluster **[fig. 7]**.

7 With one needle, pick up a 15º seed bead, a 6mm round crystal, and a 15º. Bring the other needle up through the center of the bugles, pick up a 15º, sew through the 6mm, bring the needle back down through the center of the bugles, and pick up a 15º. Cross both needles through the opposite 3mm, tucking the 6mm and the 15ºs into the center of the bugles **[fig. 8]**.

8 Repeat step 2 twice, then repeat steps 3–7. Repeat this step until you reach the desired length. End the threads.

9 On a new 2-yd. (1.8m) piece of Fireline, center eight 11ºs. With one needle, sew back through the first 11º to form a ring. Continue around the ring, and skip every other bead to make a diamond shape. Make sure the threads are exiting the same 11º.

10 With each needle, sew through the 11ºs on either side of the end 3mm on the bottom of the bracelet **[fig. 9, a–b and aa–bb]**. This will center the end diamond loop, where the clasp will be attached.

11 With each needle, pick up an 11º, and sew through the next 11ºs **[b–c and bb–cc]**. With one needle, pick up an 11º and cross the other needle through it. With each needle, sew through the next bugles **[c–d and cc–dd]**. On each needle, pick up an 11º, and sew through the next bugle. With one needle, pick up an 11º, and cross the other needle through it **[d–e and dd–ee]**. Repeat this process along the bottom. When you reach the last unit, pick up seven 11ºs on one needle, and sew

through them with the other needle to form a ring. Sew through the beads in the ring again, skipping every other bead to mimic the diamond shape. End the threads.

12 On a new 2-yd. (1.8m) piece of Fireline, center an 11º. With each needle, sew though the first 11ºs on either side of the end 3mm on the top of the bracelet. Repeat as in step 11 along the top of the bracelet. Reinforce as needed, and end the threads.

13 Open a jump ring, and attach half of the clasp to each loop on the bottom of the bracelet.

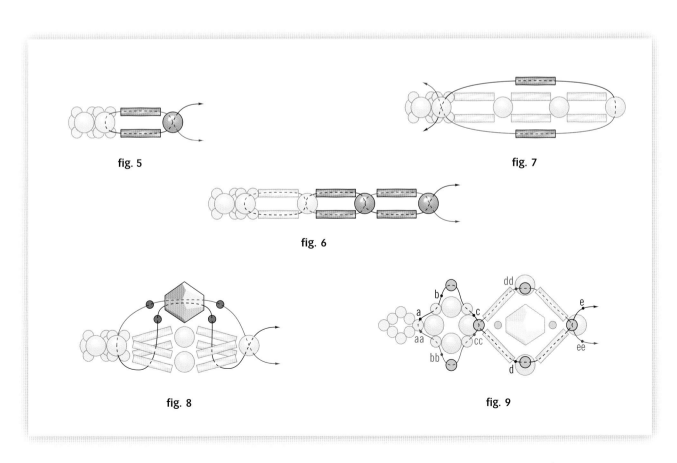

fig. 5

fig. 7

fig. 6

fig. 8

fig. 9

COLORS

Necklace

- **11** 6mm bicone crystals (Swarovski, sand opal)
- **88** 6mm twisted bugle beads (matte brown)
- 3mm crystal pearls (Swarovski, dark brown)
- 4–5 grams 11º seed beads (gold-lined AB)
- 2–3 grams 15º seed beads (brown)

Earrings

- **8** 9mm bugle beads (metallic bronze)
- **2** 8mm crystal pearls (Swarovski, white)
- **8** 3mm bicone crystals (Swarovski, sand opal)
- **18** 4mm gold-toned spacer beads
- Gram 11º seed beads (gold-lined AB)

3mm crystal

8mm pearl

4mm spacer bead

This necklace has 21 crystal components (plus one for the dangle). The earrings use slightly larger beads: 8mm pearls framed by 9mm bugles.

Basics Review

Stringing & Wirework

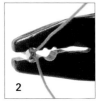

Crimping

Use crimping pliers and crimp beads to secure the ends of flexible beading wire:

1 Position the crimp bead in the notch closest to the handle of the crimping pliers. Hold the wires apart to make sure one wire is on each side of the dent, and squeeze the pliers to compress the crimp bead.

2 Position the crimp bead in the notch near the tip of the pliers with the dent facing the tips. Squeeze the pliers to fold the crimp in half. Tug on the wires to make sure the crimp is secure.

Opening and closing plain loops, jump rings, and earring findings

1 Hold a loop or a jump ring with two pairs of pliers.

2 To open the loop or jump ring, bring the tips of one pair of pliers toward you, and push the tips of the other pair away from you. Reverse the steps to close.

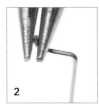

Making a plain loop

1 Using chainnose pliers, make a right-angle bend approximately ¼ in. (6mm) from the end of the wire.

2 Grip the tip of the wire with roundnose pliers. Press downward slightly, and rotate the wire into a loop. The closer to the tip of the pliers you work, the smaller the loop will be.

3 Let go, then grip the loop at the same place on the pliers, and keep turning to close the loop.

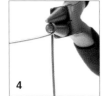

Making a wrapped loop

1 Using chainnose pliers, make a right-angle bend approximately 1¼ in. (3.2cm) from the end of the wire.

2 Position the jaws of the roundnose pliers in the bend.

3 Curve the short end of the wire over the top jaw of the pliers.

4 Reposition the pliers so the lower jaw fits snugly in the loop. Curve the wire downward around the bottom jaw of the pliers. This is the first half of a wrapped loop.

5 To complete the wraps, grasp the top of the loop with chainnose pliers.

6 Wrap the wire around the stem two or three times. Trim the excess wire, and gently press the cut end close to the wraps with chainnose pliers.

Bead Stitching

Stop bead
Use a stop bead to secure beads temporarily as you begin stitching. Choose a bead that is distinct from the beads in your project. String the stop bead, and sew through it again in the same direction. For extra security, sew through it again.

Adding and ending thread
To add a thread, sew into the beadwork several rows prior to the point where the last bead was added. Weave through the beadwork, following the existing thread path. Tie a few half-hitch knots between beads, and exit where the last stitch ended. To end a thread, weave back into the beadwork, following the existing thread path and tying two or three half-hitch knots between beads as you go. Change directions as you weave so the thread crosses itself. Sew through a few beads after the last knot, and trim the thread.

Half-hitch knot
Pass the needle under the thread between two beads. A loop will form as you pull the thread through. Cross back over the thread between the beads, sew through the loop, and pull gently to draw the knot into the beadwork.

Square knot
Bring the left-hand thread over the right-hand thread and around. Cross right over left, and go through the loop.

CHEVRON CHAIN

1 On a comfortable length of thread, attach a stop bead, leaving a 6-in. (15 cm) tail.

2 Pick up three color-A seed beads, three color-B seed beads, three As, three color-C seed beads, three As, and three Bs **[fig. 1, a–b]**. Sew back through the first three As **[b–c]**.

3 Pick up three Cs, three As, and three Bs, and sew back through the last three As added in the previous stitch **[fig. 2]**.

4 Repeat step 3 **[fig. 3]** to the desired length. The direction of the Vs will alternate with each stitch.

fig. 1 fig. 2

fig. 3

CROSSWEAVE TECHNIQUE
Crossweave is a beading technique in which you string one or more beads on both ends of a length of thread or cord and then cross the ends through one or more beads.

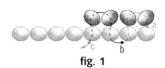

fig. 1

fig. 2

HERRINGBONE STITCH

Flat strip

1 Work the first row in ladder stitch (see "Ladder stitch: Making a ladder") to the desired length, exiting the top of the last bead added.

2 Pick up two beads, and sew down through the next bead in the previous row **[fig. 1, a–b]**. Sew up through the following bead in the previous row, pick up two beads, and sew down through the next bead **[b–c]**. Repeat across the first row.

3 To turn to start the next row, sew down through the end bead in the previous row and back through the last bead of the pair just added **[fig. 2, a–b]**. Pick up two beads, sew down through the next bead in the previous row, and sew up through the following bead **[b–c]**. Continue adding pairs of beads across the row.

4 To turn without having thread show on the edge, pick up an accent or smaller bead before you sew back through the last bead of the pair you just added, or work the "Concealed turn" below.

Concealed turn

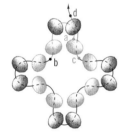

To hide the thread on the edge without adding a bead for each turn, sew up through the second-to-last bead in the previous row, and continue through the last bead added **[a–b]**. Pick up two beads, sew down through the next bead in the previous row, and sew up through the following bead **[b–c]**. Continue adding pairs of beads across the row. Using this turn will flatten the angle of the edge beads, making the edge stacks look a little different than the others.

Tubular

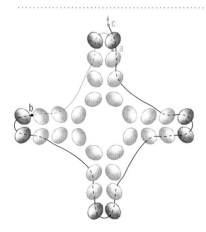

1 Work a row of ladder stitch (see "Ladder stitch: Making a ladder") to the desired length using an even number of beads. Form it into a ring to create the first round (see "Ladder stitch: Forming a ring"). Your thread should exit the top of a bead.

2 Pick up two beads, sew down through the next bead in the previous round **[a–b]**, and sew up through the following bead. Repeat to complete the round **[b–c]**.

3 You will need to step up to start the next round. Sew up through two beads — the next bead in the previous round and the first bead added in the new round **[c–d]**.

4 Continue adding two beads per stitch. As you work, snug up the beads to form a tube, and step up at the end of each round until your rope is the desired length.

Twisted tubular

1 Follow step 1 of the instructions for tubular herringbone stitch.

2 To create a twist in the tube, pick up two beads, and sew down through one bead in the next stack and up through two beads in the following stack **[a–b]**. Repeat around, adding two beads per stitch, but step up through three beads in the last repeat instead of two **[b–c]**. Snug up the beads. The twist will begin to appear after the sixth round. Continue until your rope is the desired length.

LADDER STITCH

Making a ladder

1 Pick up two beads, and sew through them both again, positioning the beads side by side so that their holes are parallel **[fig. 1, a–b]**.

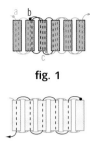

fig. 1

2 Add subsequent beads by picking up one bead, sewing through the previous bead, then sewing through the new bead **[b–c]**. Continue for the desired length.

This technique produces uneven tension, which you can correct by zigzagging back through the beads in the opposite direction **[fig. 2],** or by using the "Crossweave method" below.

fig. 2

Crossweave method

1 Thread a needle on each end of a length of thread, and center a bead.

2 Working in crossweave technique (see "Crossweave technique"), pick up a bead with one needle, and cross the other needle through it **[a–b and aa–bb]**. Add all subsequent beads in the same manner.

NETTING

Netting produces airy, flexible beadwork that resembles a net and can be worked vertically, horizontally, or in the round (tubular netting). Netting starts with a base row or round of beads upon which subsequent rows or rounds are stitched. Subsequent rows or rounds are added by picking up a given odd number of beads, and sewing through the center bead of the next stitch in the previous row or round.

Instructions for netting vary for each project, but some common variations include three-, five-, and seven-bead netting. The number of beads per stitch determines the drape of the overall piece. More beads per stitch produce larger spaces and a more fluid drape.

Tubular netting

1 Pick up 24 11ºs, and sew through them again to form a ring, exiting the first 11º picked up.

2 Pick up five 11ºs, skip five 11ºs in the ring, and sew through the next 11º in the ring **[a–b]**. Repeat to complete the round **[b–c]**. Step up through the first three 11ºs in the first stitch **[c–d]**.

3 Pick up five 11ºs, skip five 11ºs in the previous round, and sew through the center 11º in the next stitch in the previous round **[d–e]**. Repeat to complete the round, and step up through three 11ºs in the first stitch **[e–f]**.

4 Repeat step 3 to complete the sample.

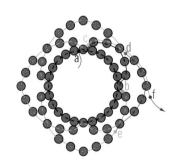

PEYOTE STITCH

Flat even-count

1 Pick up an even number of beads **[a–b]**. These beads will shift to form the first two rows.

2 To begin row 3, pick up a bead, skip the last bead picked up in the previous step, and sew back through the next bead **[b–c]**. For each stitch, pick up a bead, skip a bead in the previous row, and sew through the next bead, exiting the first bead picked up **[c–d]**. The beads added in this row are higher than the previous rows and are referred to as "up-beads."

3 For each stitch in subsequent rows, pick up a bead, and sew through the next up-bead in the previous row **[d–e]**. To count peyote stitch rows, count the total number of beads along both straight edges.

Flat odd-count

Odd-count peyote is the same as even-count peyote, except for the turn on odd-numbered rows, where the last bead of the row can't be attached in the usual way because there is no up-bead to sew through.

Work the traditional odd-row turn as follows:

1 Begin as for flat even-count peyote, but pick up an odd number of beads. Work row 3 as in even-count, stopping before adding the last two beads.

2 Work a figure-8 turn at the end of row 3: Pick up the next-to-last bead (#7), and sew through #2, then #1 **[a–b]**. Pick up the last bead of the row (#8), and sew through #2, #3, #7, #2, #1, and #8 **[b–c]**.

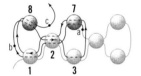

fig. 1

You can work this turn at the end of each odd-numbered row, but this edge will be stiffer than the other. Instead, in subsequent odd-numbered rows, pick up the last bead of the row, then sew under the thread bridge immediately below. Sew back through the last bead added to begin the next row.

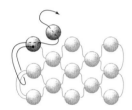

fig. 2

Circular

Circular peyote is also worked in continuous rounds like tubular peyote, but the rounds stay flat and radiate outward from the center as a result of increases or using larger beads. If the rounds do not increase, the beadwork will become tubular.

Tubular

Tubular peyote stitch follows the same stitching pattern as flat peyote, but instead of sewing back and forth, you work in rounds.

1 Start with an even number of beads in a ring.

2 Sew through the first bead in the ring. Pick up a bead, skip a bead in the ring, and sew through the next bead. Repeat to complete the round.

3 You need to step up to be in position for the next round. Sew through the first bead added in round 3. Pick up a bead, and sew through the second bead in round 3. Repeat to achieve the desired length.

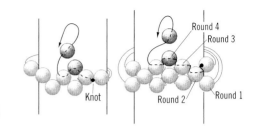

Zipping up or joining

To zip up (join) two sections of a flat peyote piece invisibly, match up the two end rows and zigzag through the up-beads on both ends.

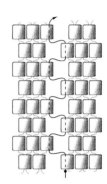

RIGHT-ANGLE WEAVE

Flat strip

1 To start the first row of right-angle weave, pick up four beads, and tie them into a ring (see "Square knot"). Sew through the first three beads again.

2 Pick up three beads. Sew through the last bead in the previous stitch **[a–b]**, and continue through the first two beads picked up in this stitch **[b–c]**.

3 Continue adding three beads per stitch until the first row is the desired length. You are stitching in a figure-8 pattern, alternating the direction of the thread path for each stitch.

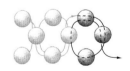

Forming a strip into a ring

Exit the end bead of the last stitch, pick up a bead, and sew through the end bead of the first stitch. Pick up a bead, and sew through the end bead of the last stitch. Retrace the thread path to reinforce the join.

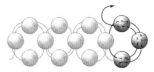

fig. 1

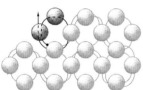

fig. 2

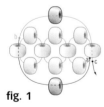

fig. 3

fig. 4

RIGHT-ANGLE WEAVE (CONTINUED)

Adding rows

1 To add a row, sew through the last stitch of row 1, exiting an edge bead along one side **[fig. 1]**.

2 Pick up three beads, and sew through the edge bead your thread exited in the previous step **[fig. 2, a–b]**. Continue through the first new bead **[b–c]**.

3 Pick up two beads, and sew back through the next edge bead in the previous row and the bead your thread exited at the start of this step **[fig. 3, a–b]**. Continue through the two new beads and the following edge bead in the previous row **[b–c]**.

4 Pick up two beads, and sew through the last two beads your thread exited in the previous stitch and the first new bead. Continue working a figure-8 thread path, picking up two beads per stitch for the rest of the row **[fig. 4]**.

Tubular

1 Work a flat strip of right-angle weave that is one stitch shorter than needed for the desired circumference of the tube. Form the strip into a ring, exiting an edge bead in the connecting stitch.

2 Add rounds, picking up three beads in the first stitch, two beads in the subsequent stitches, and one bead in the final stitch to join the first and last stitches in the round.

Cubic

In cubic right-angle weave, each cube has six surfaces—four sides, a top, and a bottom. Each surface is made up of four beads, but since the beads are shared, 12 beads are used to make the first cube, and only eight beads are used for each cube thereafter.

To begin the first cube, work three right-angle weave stitches. Join the first and last stitches to form a ring: Pick up a bead, sew through the end bead in the first stitch **[fig. 1, a–b]**, pick up a bead, and sew through the end bead in the last stitch **[b–c]**.

Fig. 2 shows a three-dimensional view of the resulting cube. To make the cube more stable, sew through the four beads on the top of the cube **[fig. 3]**. Sew through the beadwork to the bottom of the cube, and sew through the four remaining beads.

ST. PETERSBURG CHAIN

Single

1 Attach a stop bead to a comfortable length of thread.

2 Pick up six color-A seed beads. Sew through the third and fourth As again, so the fifth and sixth beads form an adjacent column **[fig. 1]**.

3 Pick up a color-B seed bead, and sew back through the next three As in the column **[fig. 2]**.

4 Pick up a B, and sew through the two As in the newest column **[fig. 3]**.

5 Pick up four As, and sew through the first two As just picked up, sliding the four beads tight to the existing chain **[fig. 4]**.

6 Pick up a B, and sew back through the next three As in the column **[fig. 5]**.

7 Pick up a B, and sew through the two As in the new column **[fig. 6]**.

8 Repeat steps 5–7 to the desired length.

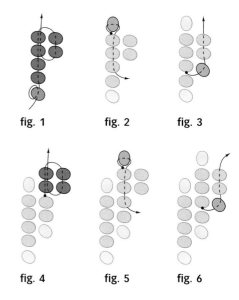

fig. 1　　　fig. 2　　　fig. 3

fig. 4　　　fig. 5　　　fig. 6

Double

1 Attach a stop bead at the center of 2 yd. (1.8m) of thread. Wind one half of the thread on a card or bobbin, so it stays out of the way as you work the first half of the chain.

2 Work as in steps 2–8 of "Single St. Petersburg chain" until the band is the desired length. Attach a stop bead to temporarily secure the thread.

3 Remove the stop bead from the starting end of the chain. Pick up six As, and sew through the third and fourth As again **[fig. 1]**.

4 Pick up a B, and sew back through the next three As in the column **[fig. 2]**.

5 Sew through the adjacent B from the first side of the chain and the two As in the newest column of the second side **[fig. 3]**. Pull tight.

6 Pick up four As, and sew through the first two As again. Pick up a B, and sew back through the next three As in the column. Sew through the next B in the first chain and through the two As in the newest column **[fig. 4]**. Repeat this step to the end of the chain.

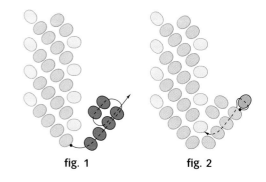

fig. 1　　　　　fig. 2

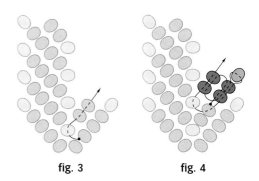

fig. 3　　　　　fig. 4

FRINGE

Fringe is often used as embellishment along the edge or surface of beadwork. The number and sizes of beads you pick up determine the length of each fringe.

To work fringe, pick up as many beads as desired for the length of the fringe, skip the last bead picked up, and sew back through the beads just picked up **[fig. 1]**. To add a picot to the fringe end, pick up the desired number of beads, skip the last three beads picked up, and sew back through the beads just picked up **[fig. 2]**.

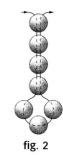

fig. 1　　　　　fig. 2

Colors

Crystal 001
White Opal 234
White Alabaster 281
Rose Water Opal 395
Rosaline 508
Vintage Rose 319
Light Rose 223
Rose 209
Indian Pink 289
Fuchsia 502
Ruby 501
Padparadscha 542
Rose Peach 262
Sun 248
Fireopal 237
Hyacinth 236
Light Siam 227
Siam 208
Garnet 241
Burgundy 515
Amethyst 204
Cyclamen Opal 398
Light Amethyst 212
Violet 371
Provence Lavender 283
Tanzanite 539

Purple Velvet 277
Dark Indigo 288
Montana 207
Denim Blue 266
Capri Blue 243
Sapphire 206
Light Sapphire 211
Air Blue Opal 285
Aquamarine 202
Light Azore 361
Indian Sapphire 217
Pacific Opal 390
Light Turquoise 263
Mint Alabaster 397
Turquoise 267
Indicolite 379
Caribbean Blue Opal 394
Blue Zircon 229
Chrysolite 238
Crysolite Opal 294
Peridot 214
Fern Green 291
Erinite 360
Emerald 205
Palace Green Opal 393
Olivine 228

Khaki 550
Sunflower 292
Light Topaz 226
Citrine 249
Jonquil 213
Silk 391
Light Peach 362
Sand Opal 287
Light Colorado Topaz 246
Topaz 203
Light Smoked Topaz 221
Smoked Topaz 220
Mocca 286
Smoky Quartz 225
Greige 284
Light Grey Opal 383
Black Diamond 215
Jet 280

Effects

Crystal Aurore Boreale 001 AB
Crystal Aurore Boreale 2x 001 AB2
Crystal Satin 001 SAT
Crystal Comet Argent Light 001 CAL
Crystal Matt Finish 001 MAT
Crystal Moonlight 001 MOL
Crystal Silver Shade 001 SSHA

Crystal Luminous Green 001 LUMG
Crystal Golden Shadow 001 GSHA
Crystal Copper 001 COP
Crystal Astral Pink 001 API
Crystal Red Magma 001 REDM
Crystal Antique Pink 001 ANTP
Crystal Blue Shade 001 BLSH
Crystal Bermuda Blue 001 BBL
Crystal Heliotrope 001 HEL
Crystal Metallic Blue 2x 001 METBL2
Crystal Vitrail Light 001 VL
Crystal Vitrail Medium 001 VM
Crystal Tabac 001 TAB
Crystal Metallic Light Gold 2x 001 MLG2
Crystal Bronze Shade 001 BRSH
Crystal Dorado 2x 001 DOR2
Jet Nut 2x 280 NUT2
Crystal Silver Night 001 SINI
Jet Hematite 280 HEM
Jet Hematite 2x 280 HEM2

Crystal Blend Colors

Burgundy-Blue Zircon Blend 001 723
Amethyst Blend 001 721
Fern Green-Topaz Blend 001 724
Topaz Blend 001 722

XILION Bead
Art. 5328

Classic Colors
Exclusive Colors

WWW.CREATE-YOUR-STYLE.COM

About *Anna*

Anna Elizabeth Draeger is a well-known jewelry designer, former associate editor for *Bead&Button* magazine, and the author of *Crystal Brilliance* and *Great Designs for Shaped Beads*. Since 2009, Anna has been an ambassador for the *Create Your Style* with Swarovski Elements program, a handpicked worldwide network of artists who are known for their design expertise and passion for teaching.

Reach Anna via email at beadbiz@mac.com, or visit her website: originaldesignsbyanna@squarespace.com

Acknowledgments

Being a Create Your Style *Ambassador is a great honor. I am part of an elite group of designers who were chosen to represent the products and Swarovski brand through our designs, as well as our love of all things sparkly! Swarovski often sponsors classes and books to help spread the word about their wonderful products, and I am so pleased that this book bears their brand.*

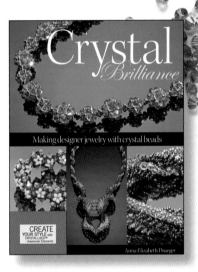
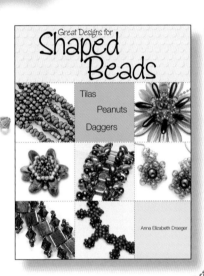